P9-BYU-562

Blessed Are the Bored in Spirit
A Young Catholic's Search for Meaning

MARK HART

SERVANT BOOKS

PUBLISHED BY ST. ANTHONY MESSENGER PRESS
CINCINNATI, OHIO

English translation of the *Catechism of the Catholic Church* for the United States of America Copyright ©1994, United States Catholic Conference, Inc.—Libreria Editrice Vaticana. English translation of the: *Catechism of the Catholic Church Modifications from the Editio Typica* Copyright ©1997, United States Catholic Conference, Inc.—Libreria Editrice Vaticana. Used with permission.

Unless otherwise noted, Scripture passages have been taken from the *Revised Standard Version,* Catholic edition. Copyright ©1946, 1952, 1971 by the Division of Christian Education of the National Council of the Churches of Christ in the USA. Used by permission. All rights reserved.

Cover design by John Lucas
Cover photo © Fotostudio FM/zefa/Corbis
Book design by Mark Sullivan

LIBRARY OF CONGRESS CATALOGING-IN-PUBLICATION DATA
Hart, Mark, 1973-
  Blessed are the bored in spirit : a young Catholic's search for meaning / Mark Hart.
     p. cm.
  ISBN 0-86716-677-0 (pbk. : alk. paper) 1. Hart, Mark, 1973- 2. Catholics—Biography. I. Title.

BX4705.H32A3 2006
282.092—dc22

                                        2006002555

ISBN-13 978-0-86716-677-4
ISBN-10 0-86716-677-0
Copyright ©2006 Mark Hart. All rights reserved.

Published by Servant Books, an imprint of
St. Anthony Messenger Press.
28 W. Liberty St.
Cincinnati, OH 45202
www.AmericanCatholic.org

Printed in the United States of America.

Printed on acid-free paper.

06 07 08 09 10 5 4 3 2

DEDICATION

Melanie
Sweetheart, you are my best friend.
I am left humbled by your prayer
and speechless by your beauty.
Thank you for loving me as Christ does.
Words cannot express my love for you.

CONTENTS

Introduction
1

Chapter One
Crashing to Earth: Conversion 101 / 5

Chapter Two
Dumb as an Oxymoron: The Fear of the Lord / 21

Chapter Three
Mass Chaos: A Holy Day of Opportunity / 37

Chapter Four
Body Building: Tearing Down Our Temples / 51

Chapter Five
Reconciling Your Issues: Thinking Inside the Box / 63

Chapter Six
Recreational Sex: Living in the Flesh / 77

Chapter Seven
Finding Courage in Suffering: Blood, Sweat and Tears / 95

Chapter Eight
Student Counsel: More Than a Popularity Contest / 105

Chapter Nine
Catholicism: The Never-Ending Crossword / 117

Notes
129

I WAS BORN, BAPTIZED AND RAISED ROMAN CATHOLIC. I come from a family of six kids that never missed a holy day. I went to parochial school, but I do not fear penguins. I knew where our family Bible was kept, but I never read it. I knew who the saints were, but I sure didn't want to be one.

I knew we got ashes on Ash Wednesday and couldn't eat meat on Fridays before Easter. I knew how to light the incense (as part of my altar boy duties) but couldn't figure out why they would give open flames to little boys in flowing robes. I could tell you all of my sins, but not why they were wrong. I went to Mass because that is what Catholics do.

I knew I was a Catholic, but when I got to college, I began to wonder what difference it really made, and I wondered if I even wanted to remain one. I wanted to debate teachings and discuss thoughts and questions, but I didn't know where to begin. My situation was not unique.

I was a postmodern Catholic.

I still am a postmodern Catholic.

I am a young Catholic. I want to live as a good Catholic Christian. I still live in the world, but don't want to be a mindless product of the world. I don't have all the answers; I'm just sorting through the questions.

The numbers don't lie. A majority of Catholics disagree with fundamental, doctrinal teachings of the Church. Many cite the Church's "refusal to change" as primary reason for their disagreement. Fifty weeks a year, the churches are not full.

The pews are emptying because the truth of Christ has been forfeited, too often, on altars of conformity, funded by the court of comfort and public opinion. The pews are emptying because the reality of sin has taken on an almost fairy-tale-like existence in our world today. The pews are emptying because where there is no sin, there is no need of a Savior.

At the same time, the truth in the twenty-first century is that everyone with a phone, a car, a computer, a radio or a television has lost the "excuse of ignorance" when it comes to God. Whether or not a person was fortunate enough to be raised in a faithful family, nearly all have encountered the messages of Jesus in artwork, on the airwaves, in churches or on street corners. It's not always lovingly uttered, but the name of Jesus is out there. People can ask a question or open a book. Many choose not to. Some fear it. Others don't care. Still others are self-consumed. Many choose ignorance because it seems easier or safer. For many people, "less knowledge = less responsibility."

God is rich in mercy and unyielding in passion, but God is not a pushover. He knows not only what we have heard or learned in our lifetime, but also what we chose not to hear, learn or ponder. Ignorance is not the best policy. Everyone, regardless of his position with God, needs to ask the question, "Who is Jesus?" and "What do I believe?" These questions have huge ramifications. Those who choose ignorance will live empty lives, and their afterlife becomes very uncertain. It's not ignorant or foolish to believe in life after death, or in a God who loves you. It's far more ignorant to believe that money, fame or the things of this world are all that this life has to offer.

Young people fear commitment. They want to belong, but not to stay long. They want to count, but too few stand to be counted. They want to be heard, but are reluctant to speak. It has become more important to be liked than respected, to be tolerant than to be truthful. So, to remain on everyone's good side, many people (Christians included) don't sell out for God. People play games with God, picking and choosing the teachings they want to follow or the truths they want to believe. They live as though they haven't heard of him, and act as though they've never heard of his consequences: the "wages of sin," the punishment. The cafeteria of Catholic doctrine is open, and millions comfortably grab for trays.

If you say that Jesus is not God, there is no reason for us to talk anymore. After all, there is money to be made, commitment-less sex to be had and people waiting to be stepped on. If Jesus isn't God, then the Bible is a sham, our creed is a myth, salvation a joke and the Church an empire of mind control.

3

If one says that Jesus is God, however, things change. Our perspective changes. Our approach changes. Everything changes the minute that we confess and profess that Jesus is Lord. Only in Jesus does pain and suffering have a purpose. Only in God is our future filled with hope and peace.

In the next nine chapters we are going to take a look at the modern spiritual journey. The themes are common: fear, sex, guilt, family, marriage, joy, suffering, school, work—and how you might need to change in one or several of these areas in order to encounter God more fully. Many people are reluctant to change, but refusing to do so is not consistent with the Christian calling. In an effort to take a more hands-on, practical look at our lives and what might be inhibiting our growth, we are going to focus on three things that might need to change within ourselves:

1. Our perspective
2. Our approach
3. Our self-offering

How is this twenty-first century generation, our generation, supposed to relate to Jesus Christ and the teachings of his Church on earth? Let's find out.

Do you say that you love God? Loving the Lord and allowing him to be the Lord of your life are two very different things.

Are you willing to change?

CHAPTER ONE

Crashing to Earth: Conversion 101

PASSENGERS FREAKED. OXYGEN MASKS DROPPED DOWN. Lights flickered. Children cried. The cabin lost power. The plane lost altitude. The attendant masked her obvious fear with a fainthearted, "Everything is under control." The pilot, too, lied through his teeth over the microphone—until it cut out mid-sentence.

Just like that, denominational boundaries ceased to exist. Everyone, it seemed, made the Sign of the Cross or variations thereof. Maybe they weren't all doing it correctly, but I can't imagine that God was going to grade anyone too hard on "right to left" or "left to right."

It was a roller coaster of emotion for the next several minutes as we rapidly lost altitude and prepared for an emergency landing. The electrical system flickered on and off in the main cabin. I buried my face in my hands and prepared to meet Jesus. How did I get to this point? in my life? in my faith? on this plane?

Just a "Plane" Old Mornin'

The sun had broken through my bedroom window that morning, unwelcome. The alarm clock radio spewed out the same inane drivel I had come to expect from morning disc jockeys. I had dragged my corpus to the bathroom and stared into the mirror eyeing a creation only God could love. Sheet marks separated the top and bottom halves of my face. The crust in the corners of my eyes cracked and fell, and my breath could have killed a rhinoceros. It was a typical morning. I was overtired, and to make things worse, I had to hurry to catch a plane.

I arrived at the airport to face the usual unpleasantries of crowds and lines, each person acting more superior than the next. Stressed-out business people competed on their cell phones to see whose conversation would reveal the most demanding and important job. The competition took a dramatic turn when one executive, apparently nervous about his impending flight, vomited while standing in line. A member of the airport janitorial staff quickly came to the rescue and purged the offending stench. The question about who had the most important job had now received a definitive answer: the janitor.

The overburdened airport security squad moved at a glacial pace. Meanwhile, the man in front of me apparently had overslept and had decided that a Monday-morning shower was optional.

Yes, I was in a bad mood. But after all, I hadn't had my coffee yet. Isn't it disconcerting that we so easily say, "I haven't had my coffee yet" to excuse a myriad of sins, from rudeness to indignation? But I was thankful for that loophole this particular morning.

After the airline gate crew cattle-prodded us onto the plane, I fought for the overhead space that my discounted Web fare clearly did not deserve. Then I sank into the seat and immediately wondered what on earth could be less comfortable than this seat—the foldout bed in my grandparents' den, maybe, or some medieval torture device?

The flight attendant did the little puppet show I had seen a thousand times. The child next to me asked me 1,214 questions between the time we pushed back from the gate and hit our cruising altitude. At this point, I noticed that the latch on the bathroom door was faulty, leaving the door to strike the doorplate with annoying rhythm. I made a mental note to refuse the mysterious processed egg food the sky waitress offered as "breakfast."

Impatiently, I awaited that glorious "ding" that alerts passengers that they can move about the cabin or access their electronic devices and drift off into a sleep-deprived coma, entertained by their favorite forms of media.

Why do I remember all the details of this morning so vividly? It wasn't because of the freshness of the peanuts. In the moment normally reserved for the "ding," a quite different sound greeted us. It was loud and jolting, like a semi that had plowed into a yak at ninety miles per hour on the freeway. It struck fear into everyone on board.

It was then that I buried my face in my hands and prepared to meet Jesus. Those who have had near-death experiences often say that their whole life flashed before their eyes. Not me, at least not at first. My life didn't flash before my eyes; random thoughts did. Who will feed my dogs? I wondered. I didn't call Mom back, I recalled. Did I throw that load in the dryer? Maybe it was just a defense mechanism. But a profound, thought-provoking time it was not.

That is, not until I thought about looking into Jesus' eyes. Then, gripped by sadness, not fear, I felt my soul get ripped open. My mind reached back not to my unaccomplished goals but rather to my accomplished sins. All the ways that I had mistreated others and mistreated myself before I "got into my faith," all that sin came rushing back with a force I had never before known.

I uttered the profoundest and sincerest prayer I had ever directed toward my Creator: "God, I'm sorry. I'm so sorry for the man I was before I really knew you."

It was so tangible, so real. It was authentic. It encompassed all I had felt during years of going through the motions in my Catholic faith when I was searching for God. It included every way I had fallen short and everything I had done wrong. All of this came to the forefront. I was sure a more perfect prayer would never cross my lips.

Fifteen seconds later, I proved myself wrong. Something clicked in my soul and a tear welled in my right eye. Clenching my teeth and swallowing a volleyball of emotion, I then uttered a more perfect prayer, the most humbling of my young life: "Lord, I am so sorry for the man I have been since I have known you."

There it was. I had let the cat out of the bag and chased it down. There was no more hiding from my sin, no more claiming ignorance or justifying selfishness. There I was in all my failure, with all of my excuses; there I was in all of my selfish glory and sin. All those dots were finally connected.

Suddenly, the unending homilies that had never captured my attention and yet had become obscurely etched in my head started to make sense. Those times I put me first and God second, thinking he wouldn't notice, rushed to the forefront. Those moments of selfishness, when I used my talents for my own gain and glory rather than for God, became clear to me. I realized all of the ways I had used and misused my body, and misused others, all in an effort to attain the one thing I could never attain without God: true joy.

That prayer time was more jolting to me than touching down on the runway with faulty landing gear. It was more real than inching through the terminal besieged by airline and emergency personnel. The worst morning of my earthly life had just become the greatest morning of my heavenly quest.

The morning of the crash landing holds an important place in my memory and a practical place in my faith life. It was memorable less for the details surrounding the excitement on board than for the revelation I had about myself. I was not stressed by the events. God's grace had a lot to do with that. I was a "good person" by most standards. I made it to Mass. I got to confession here and there. I tried to follow God, tried to do what was right, treated people fairly and did my best to be nice. I didn't cheat on my girlfriend, my taxes or my time sheet.

That comfort was my downfall. I fell into the trap. I thought that going to church and being a good person were all that God wanted from me. I was wrong. That morning on the plane I received one of God's greatest gifts—perspective.

Conversion Theory

Remember when you were a kid and the snooze button was your best friend? Maybe after you took two or three taps to the snooze followed by a couple of vicious slaps, your mom would yell to you. Ten minutes later she'd yell again. Finally, she'd pop in and give you the time (always five minutes later than it actually was). As a last resort, she'd shake you until you sat up and promised that you were awake. That final jolt was the last step in the painful process meant to get you up to join the living.

Well, the truth was that the crash landing didn't wake me up; it was the final step in an arduous journey that had begun years before. That morning was the jolt I needed in the ongoing process that carried me beyond conversion.

People talk freely about their conversion. You can hear them on Christian radio stations. You can see them on the Christian cable channels. Have you ever noticed that most conversion stories have the horrible-sinner-to-amazing-saint twist, a change so vast that even that of Jekyll and Hyde pales in comparison? Have you ever felt that your own story lacked that kind of dramatic intensity, and then questioned the sincerity of your conversion?

But the goal of the Christian life is far more than ceasing destructive or sinful behaviors. The goal is surrender to God. In that surrender, we receive the grace to abandon a life of selfishness and embrace a life of selflessness. To my thinking, that's the difference between conversion to Christ, which often primarily involves the mind, and transformation in Christ, which involves action—a change in environment, speech, conduct and motivation.

Conversions are wonderful in that they lead sinful people to become good people or at least better people. But the harsh truth is that Jesus isn't calling you to be a good person. Jesus Christ is calling you to be a new person, a new creation (Galatians 2:20), not just converted in mind but transformed in body and spirit. That means admitting that the life you currently lead might not be the life you're called to lead. It means acknowledging that there are areas of your life in which you won't let the Lord be the Lord.

Many people have conversion experiences but never put in the effort that allows true change to take root. The morning of the crash pointed me, finally, toward the true goal—transformation.

Transformation: More Than Meets the Eye

Conversion moments often lack the deep-seated motivation that allows a person to sustain change over a lifetime. That motivation is where conversion gives way to transformation. When we embrace change for a who (God) and not for a what (religion), the sacrifice takes on assurance, joy and longevity. If your transformation is rooted in a relationship with God, it can brave the unexpected storms of life.

My cradle-Catholic life was one of formation. That formation was wonderful but did little more than teach me the "rules" of God. Although I didn't always obey the rules, I inherited a general sense of morality and discipline. My formation taught me how not to live; it didn't teach me how to live in his love, transformed.

To be transformed by Christ means to be re-made and re-created by him. It takes a personal encounter. It doesn't have to be a huge watershed moment in which you are left with no alternative, although it might be. Most people wait for such a moment. But that's like saying, "I'll follow you, God, but only when my life gets so unmanageable that I cannot pull myself out alone."

What a sad commentary on human pride. Why should it take intense suffering or tragedy to turn our full attention to God? Why must it take divorce or disease or bankruptcy or addiction for us to wake up and give God permission to be in charge? Many of us desperately need a change of perspective.

In a personal encounter with God, our vision of him changes but, more importantly, the way we relate to him changes. For example, as Catholics we experience face-to-face encounters with God's grace most specifically in the sacraments. Are the sacraments personal and life-altering for you? For me, they didn't used to be. I had been formed to participate in the sacraments but not transformed so that I yearned for them. Rather than leaving me breathless with anticipation, the sacraments left me yawning, anticipating boredom. You, too, may be a product of similar formation. Meanwhile, transformation glows on the horizon like a sunrise.

What's Your Story?

The gift I received on the plane that Monday morning was the same gift that some people receive in a pew one Sunday morning, or during an AA meeting some Wednesday night, or after getting fired, or after sitting and worrying in an emergency room all night. It's the gift of self-awareness.

Self-awareness is vital for a conversion to trigger transformation. When all the masks of self-importance fade away, when the "good person" goal falls to the wayside, when all you are left with is the authentic you, then you can start being who God calls you to be. But what does that mean on a practical level?

My story is different from yours, but not much. The details differ but my story, like yours, is the story of Scripture. God created me and I sinned. I then had to be humble enough to admit it, seek forgiveness and not "move on" but move forward toward him.

God created you and you have sinned. Where is your current movement taking you? Don't get caught in the conversion trap thinking that ceasing a behavior equals love of God. Acknowledge where you are and consider where you are not.

On the Road, Again...for the First Time

Let's take a look at one person who did just that sort of self-evaluation. Unfortunately, when we hear the story of Saint Paul's conversion proclaimed at Mass, we often go into a mental coma. It's one of those "I get the gist of it" passages. We know the principal characters and basic premise, but we overlook the practical and life-challenging details.

> But Saul, still breathing threats and murder against the disciples of the Lord...approached Damascus, and suddenly a light from heaven flashed about him. And he fell to the ground and heard a voice saying to him, "Saul, Saul, why do you persecute me?" And he said, "Who are you, Lord?" And he said, "I am Jesus, whom you are

persecuting; but rise and enter the city, and you will be told what you are to do." The men who were traveling with him stood speechless, hearing the voice but seeing no one. Saul arose from the ground; and when his eyes were opened, he could see nothing....And for three days he was without sight, and neither ate nor drank. (Acts 9:1–9)

Saul was a devout Jew with an excellent education, strong, passionate, charismatic and embittered. Based on his drive and skills alone, he would have had what it takes to rise to the top of corporate America. Saul would have been on the cover of *Forbes* magazine by age thirty and touted as the up-and-comer by every publication.

When Saul encountered God face-to-face, his journey took a turn. All of a sudden, the up-and-comer was coming up short. The beauty of it was that God acted in front of other people, leaving Saul's peers without doubt and leaving Saul without excuses. No way could he mistake this for a migraine or midlife crisis; he couldn't explain this one away. Humbled, broken and literally blinded, he needed help, time and a change in perspective.

Those three days must have been overwhelming for Saul. Far more than a morning of "snoozing," the sheets had been ripped from his bed. Sure, he was blind to the world, but for the first time he was seeing 20/20. Left with nothing to see outside of himself, he had to look within. He must not have liked what he saw, for he wasn't just converted in his beliefs, he was transformed in his soul. His new name, Paul, signified a change in his essence.

The hardest road a person will ever travel is the road from his head to his heart. Saul, on a literal road to Damascus, made his way into the city. Then he made that far more difficult inward journey. You are called to make that inward journey, too. You are, like Paul, a beloved child of God. You, too, have had experiences of God's call. They might not have had the flash or the dazzle of Saul's, but the root of the encounter and God's reason for it are the same— to help you know him and serve him.

Do you sometimes feel that God the Father must have known the people in Scripture more intimately than he knows you? If so, pray through the following verses.

> Before I formed you in the womb I knew you, / and before you were born I consecrated you. (Jeremiah 1:5)

> For I know the plans I have for you, says the Lord, plans for welfare and not for evil, to give you a future and a hope. Then you will call upon me and come and pray to me, and I will hear you. (Jeremiah 29:11–12)

Commit these verses to memory. Write about them in your journal. Reflect on them. Put them on the fridge or tape them to the mirror in your bathroom. Doesn't it sound like God has a specific plan for you?

You might think, "I'm too big a sinner for God to use me." Think again. You might say, "If I encountered Christ face to face, and heard his voice, I'd change, too." But don't you hear his voice? Don't you hear his word in Scripture? You consume Christ every Sunday. How much more intimate can you get? You encounter Christ more fully and directly than Saul did and his encounter radically transformed his life and turned him into a preacher of the Word who spent the rest of his life teaching and praying and preaching in spite of being shipwrecked, stoned, whipped, caned, imprisoned and left for dead. (See 2 Corinthians 11.)

What has your encounter done for the world?...Yeah, me too. Don't get too down on yourself.

Grounded in Reality

Ask yourself what's stopping you from setting the world ablaze for God. Could it be your reluctance to surrender to him? Keep in mind that Satan doesn't want you to succeed. Yes, evil is real and the devil is real. If you have ever felt you are too sinful for God to love or to use, already you have fallen victim to the evil one. As soon as you feel that you have less to offer than you really do, already his foot is in the door.

So how do I know that God wants to use you? That's the beauty of Scripture. It reminds us of God's timeless truths: He chose to use a murderer like Saul. He can use you and me and anybody else who surrenders to him and his persistent love.

Here's the truth about Saul. He knew his religion, worshiped regularly, quoted Scripture and spoke freely about those who seemed to be straying from the faith. Many Christians today are like Saul. They head to their houses of worship on the Sabbath, they know their "law" and they judge others. How ironic that Saul used the law to justify his genocide, when the Commandments clearly state, "Thou shalt not kill." And he planned more bloodshed in Damascus before he was knocked to the ground.

The ground—that's interesting. It was out of the ground—the clay, *adamah* in Hebrew—that God formed Adam. It was out of the mud that Christ brought sight to the blind man (see John 9), and it was on the ground that the soon-to-be greatest missionary apostle would have his life-changing encounter with God. The Latin word for earth or ground is *humus*, from which we derive the word "humility." Indeed, to be a person of humility we must first be grounded. Basically, to be transformed we must be brought down to earth, like it or not.

Practically Speaking

How do we get to that place of humility, that place where God can use us? By being open to God. As you consider your degree of openness, ask yourself how you envision God. As a judge? As a father? What needs to change in your life in order to change your perspective?

Maybe you're waiting for a sign. My crash landing wasn't my initial wake-up call; it was my "stop running" call. It was my parent pulling the sheets off the bed and saying, "I'm glad you're not worse, but you could be so much better."

Why wait for some burning bush moment with God? Why stall by saying, "Well, if God really wants me to do something, all he has to do is tell me"? Yes, the Lord does work in mysterious ways, but most of the time he works in very obvious, everyday ways.

Tonight, leave the television off. Log off the computer. Sit in silence. Go to bed early. Take time to reflect on all the ways that the Lord has already tried to get through to you.

God is active in your life. How receptive are you to his advances?

Take time to write out how you see God. Maybe it will be all adjectives. Perhaps it will be images. You might fill pages with paragraphs or your page might contain only sentence fragments. Once you've created your list, spend some time in prayer. Following prayer, take a new page and write out how God sees you. Let his words and phrases flow through your pen. When you're finished, compare the two; if they are too similar that probably means your vision of either yourself or of God is not completely realistic.

Take three days, as Saul did, and participate in activities that could help you mature in your understanding of God. Get out to nature and go for a hike. Head to the tallest building you can find and take in the view. Rather than hitting that snooze button, set the alarm earlier and welcome the sunrise with only God and coffee to keep you company.

If you want something you have never had, you must be willing to do something that you have never done. If you want to change your perspective of the Creator of the world, do something to change the world around you. You might think that a "transformation" is a lifetime away, but it's not. Conversions become everyday experiences. With each conversion comes an opportunity to finally stop the merry-go-round life that you control and get in line for the roller coaster that he controls.

Your transformation doesn't have to begin with an emergency landing, the blare of an ambulance siren, the flatline of a heart monitor or the cocking of a trigger. It can begin with the opening of your eyes and heart to God's presence in the midst of class, work, rush hour or even a seemingly drab, uninteresting Sunday Mass during Ordinary Time. Make it a point, several times a day, to stop what you are doing and "find" God around you. Pick a moment, such as when you look at your watch, and make that a "God moment." Notice his presence in the obvious things like family pictures on your desk, or the not-so-obvious things like the mess of dishes in the sink—yet another day that he provided your family with food to eat.

As you practice these little exercises, you'll see God's generosity more clearly and know his presence more deeply. Your change in perspective will contribute to your inner transformation. Even with the proper perspective, however, the work is just beginning. The next thing that often needs to change is your approach.

CHAPTER TWO

Dumb as an Oxymoron: The Fear of the Lord

JERRY SEINFELD ONCE NOTED THE FACT THAT THE #2 fear in the world is "death," while the #1 fear is "public speaking." Then he quipped, "So—at a funeral, the average person would rather be lying in the casket than delivering the eulogy."

What are you most afraid of in your life? Death? Sharks? Spiders? Finals? Taxes? Divorce? Childbirth? Interest rates? Unemployment? Infidelity? Boredom? Weight gain? Disease? Clowns? Me too. Everyone is afraid of something. Even great saints feared they didn't love God with an intense enough abandon or fervent enough desire.

Foe Real

Fear is a physical and mental phenomenon that can leave you shaking and sweating, full of stress, anxiety and nausea. Its effects are measurable and paralyzing; it is an uncontrolled controller. Fear can make you want to scream and simultaneously leave you unable to make a sound. It can make you want to run but leave you standing motionless. Both options leave you breathless. Denying the existence of fear only allows it to sink its roots deeper into your soul. The most fearful person is the one who is too proud to admit fear, rendering him or her too weak to combat it.

Take some time to list those things that you fear. Do you fear giving up control of certain situations in your life? Do you hold onto certain relationships too tightly? Do you fear letting others see beneath the masks you wear, worried that they will reject you if they really know you? Are you afraid that God will reject you?

At the same time, fear can be an ally. Fear can keep you honest. Fear can motivate you (although it usually takes a tragedy such as the death of a loved one or dilemma such as a "D" on an exam before we actually take notice).

Unfortunately, fear often becomes the tool of the devil. Fear binds us and prevents us from moving forward. It becomes a rearview mirror of spirituality, focusing our attention on past sins and failures rather than on the mercy-filled horizons of the future. As fortune-cookie theology warns, "If you do not master your fear, fear will become your master."

Fear of change inhibits many Catholics in their spiritual journey. Yet Jesus Christ calls us to shatter that fear because the entire Christian life is about learning how to surrender to God.

Nothing, not even sin, should produce in us the sort of fear that keeps us from God. I have heard people say, "I can't go to church. My sin is too great. The walls would cave in if I walked in there." That attitude reveals the soul of someone who yearns for the heavenly mercy of God while simultaneously being consumed by a worldly fear of inadequacy. But Christ didn't spend most of his earthly ministry reaching out to prostitutes, lepers, tax collectors and vagrants simply so those with the less obvious "white collar" sins might have a nice place to gather and acknowledge his presence for an hour or so every week. He welcomes everyone.

Nothing to Fear

How are we supposed to get close enough to the Almighty to really hear his voice? How is our relationship with him supposed to bloom when the Old Testament speaks of the "fear of the Lord" over fifty times? "Fear of the Lord" is even considered one of the gifts of the Holy Spirit (Isaiah 11:1–3). What is personal or inviting about the warning to approach the Lord "...with fear, with trembling" (Psalm 2:11)?

Such verses do not indicate that we should find God unapproachable. Rather, in calling us to fear God, Scripture is primarily calling us to be in awe of God, to adore him, to recognize that God is who he says he is and that we are utterly dependent on him. This is at the heart of the scriptural meaning of fear of the Lord.

Jesus came for you, the sinner. He did not come for you, the good person who is not as bad as the rest. "Wait," you might say, "the Creator of the stars, the skies and the entire universe, of every blade of grass and every drop of water, of every living being could possibly notice little ol' me?!" Yes, that's the reality.

He mounted that cross not for "humanity" but for you. He left the splendor of heaven for the dirt of earth and took on sin and death in order to destroy both for you. That is the ludicrous beauty of the cross. That's the foolishness of it (1 Corinthians 1:18–25). That is the too often misunderstood power of the cross that simultaneously destroys fear and replaces it with awe. It takes a relationship with God, however, to gain that perspective and to shift from approaching God out of fear to approaching him in awe.

"Awe, Thanks for Trying"

We, as humans, love to be wowed by things. We rise to our feet when a hitter smacks a ball five hundred feet in a baseball game or when a basketball player dunks from the free throw line. We heap accolades on actors for their performances or on passionate teachers who help us to look at our lives in a new way. We were created with the capacity for awe, with the instinct for worship.

Unfortunately, these instincts are usually focused on imperfect human creations rather than the Creator. Why doesn't the random Wednesday sunset elicit a greater reaction than the Sunday touchdown? Why doesn't daily Scripture reading intrigue us as much as reading the newspaper? Why do we fight for the back row at Mass and the front row at a rock concert?

Nowadays, movies and their special effects wow us but we don't often stand—or better yet, kneel—in awe of God. Of course, to stand in awe of God it helps to be in his presence. Do you sit before him, in his real presence in the Blessed Sacrament, and remind yourself of the awe-inspiring reality that is God? Do you kneel before him in adoration? If not, I challenge you to do so. God did not come down from heaven to dwell in a golden box but in your heart. He is a God who created not only the universe but a Father who breathed every detail of your body into existence (Psalm 139:13) and has every single hair on your head counted (Matthew 10:30).

God created you out of love, for a specific purpose. Instead of being afraid that your vocation won't make you happy or will take you down roads you'd rather not travel, you should be in awe that he has reserved a vocation specifically for you. Your joy is spiritually and divinely intertwined with your vocation from the moment of conception. If you are unhappy in your life, it might mean you haven't yet embraced your vocation.

You can only realize your true vocation if you have the right perspective on God the Father. Call to mind or list the talents that God has gifted to you. How are you using them? Thank him for them. Acknowledge them. Recognize that they came from him. That perspective gives you confidence when you approach him.

Awe-Full Friend

An autographed copy of *Dangerous Wonder* by the late Mike Yaconelli sits on my nightstand next to my Bible. It is a must-read for Christians who have ever felt stagnant in their faith. The first time I read the book, the author's understanding of contemporary Christian experience intrigued me. Then, when I met Mike, I was even more impressed by his practical holiness.

Mike taught me that awe of God doesn't mean we approach him perfectly, but rather differently. Mike lived in awe and in doing so showed me what awe looks like: He showed me that awe doesn't shudder and stand motionless, like fear does. It barrels ahead, unable to control its enthusiasm.

Mike had a unique understanding of what I call the workingman's Christ. He spent time with Jesus daily, inviting him into every corner of his life, not just the polished rooms he was proud to display. He invited Jesus into the garage; he showed him into the attic; he invited the Lord to root around in the closets of his soul, cluttered with sin, failure and shame. And the Lord dove right in.

Mike was a youth-ministry pioneer and a talented speaker and writer. But more than that, he was authentically Christian. He went home to heaven in 2003, but the effect he had on me and on many others will ripple across the years. We spent time together on only a handful of occasions, but that time was more than meaningful. He quickly transcended the category of "colleague." Mike was my friend. He boldly challenged the fear that lulls modern followers of Jesus into complacency.

In one of my favorite passages from *Dangerous Wonder*, Mike calls for an awe of God that flows from a true understanding of who God. In spite of the language, Mike isn't advocating the old fear that holds us back. Instead, he's calling us to a bold, brave faith based on the fact that our God is "no ordinary God."

> It's time for Christianity to become a place of terror again; a place where God continually has to tell us, "Fear

not;" a place where our relationship with God is not a simple belief or doctrine or theology, but the constant awareness of God's terrifying presence in our lives. The nice, nonthreatening God needs to be replaced by the God whose very presence smashes our egos into dust, burns our sin into ashes, and strips us naked to reveal the real person within...how did we end up so comfortable with God? How did our awe of God get reduced to a lukewarm appreciation of God? How did God become a pal instead of a heart-stopping presence? How can we think of Jesus without remembering His ground-shaking, thunder-crashing, stormy exit on the cross? Why aren't we continually catching our breath and saying, "This is no ordinary God!"?[1]

Modern Christians have lost or, worse yet, never found, their awe of God. If we want to live in awe we must be willing to get dirty, roll up our sleeves and deal with our sin. We must be willing to embrace the cross, not just admire it from a distance.

Mike taught me that God loves me not in spite of my messiness, but within it. It is vital to have bold, realistic, faith-filled people like Mike in our lives. It's not good enough to have people in the office, dorm or classroom with whom we can debate religion as we do politics. No, we need people around us who are lacing up their shoes and taking to the field their own Christian battle every day.

Seek out people who are actively in the game, not just standing on the sidelines, afraid to enter in. Look for people who are getting dirty playing with God and learning as they go. We all need such people on this journey to hold us accountable and to challenge our complacency with life.

Daddy Training

When have you experienced the awesomeness of God in your life? When has fear been so present you could feel it? When has sheer awe left you breathless? Have the two ever collided? The circumstances will differ for each of us, but all of us who are actively seeking to follow Christ will eventually deal with both realities. Here's how it happened for one young man.

A new father sits quietly in the freshly painted nursery of a small three-bedroom house. His wife sleeps nearby, exhausted from a day of "relaxation" at home with a newborn. As this father stares down into his daughter's face, into his own eyes, two trains of thought begin a collision course.

"Look at this beautiful creation," he thinks to himself. "This is the first perfect thing I've ever done. Whatever I thought about you before, God, it wasn't enough." That train of thought, the A-train, has begun its journey. The "A" stands for awe, and Jesus Christ sits as the engineer inviting us to jump on board and enjoy the ride. The train pulls out of the station of the heart and becomes a blur as it gains speed, ushering in hopes and expectations.

This moving snapshot slows occasionally in its celebration of life, but only long enough to reflect on the milestones, allowing the father to see just how blessed he is that a God so big would allow him to be involved in the very act of creation. That the vastness of God's love could be contained in a body so small leaves this man speechless. Her tiny heart beats upon her father's chest. God loves his children enough to grant children to them. "Awesome...simply awesome," reflects the new daddy.

But the peace of the moment is inevitably shattered by the practical fears of a money-driven world. The F-train has now left the brain. The "F" stands for fear, and the devil sits as the engineer of this train. It's a runaway train and its route is designed to derail the soul. "How am I going to do this? Now there are two lives depending on me. I'm trapped. I couldn't quit if I wanted to...."

The enemy enters the moment and snatches peace from the room. The Norman Rockwell-like portrait of hope and harmony is now reduced to an anxiety-filled blur of *anime*. "I'm not worthy of this. I don't know if I can do it." The father's heart now begins to pound. "What if I'm not cut out for this? I don't know how to take care of a baby."

The same fears he had as a single man are now heightened. Job security takes on new meaning. Medical checkups are no longer routine. The breathlessness that consumed him just weeks earlier in that delivery room has returned as the suffocating grip of insecurity. The F-train is not stopping. It rounds the bend, and both engineers' eyes meet on the tracks between heart and head. Destination? The soul.

The trains of thought seem to collide, silently derailing within him. He whispers the most sincere prayer of the day, "God, please don't let me screw this up." At once, everything stops. The air in the room is still. Life pauses as if, for a split second, God's remote control has frozen everything within the frame.

Before another thought can leave the father's mind, his daughter lightly exhales. One single breath from the beautiful creature and hope is restored. God has pressed "play" on his universal remote with the gentle kiss of life, a single breath. Motion returns and the sounds of life come cascading back.

There was a breathless impact, an everlasting impact, on the tracks of the young father's life.

This story is as old as Christianity itself. God is always waiting to expel doubts and calm our hearts. We can imagine, for example, that the trains of fear and awe also collided one night under a Middle Eastern sky.

Not Your Average Joe

Saint Joseph went from being a wood- and stoneworker in the forgotten backwater town of Nazareth to being the most important and prominent stepfather in the history of humanity. Did the trains of awe and fear collide on the tracks of Joseph's soul on any of those frigid nights in a Bethlehem cave? Did the A- and F-trains bear down on one another under the starry night sky? I believe they did. What went through Joseph's heart the night of Jesus' birth as he looked into his eyes and realized, possibly for the first time, his unfathomable vocation to raise God's Son as his own?

Joseph's fears would have stemmed from his own sense of sin and human inadequacy. He knew the fear of fatherhood and the uncertainty that comes with it. He realized, with a father's heart, his desire and duty to provide for his family members, to protect them and safeguard them from pain. In his book, *Heart of Darkness*, author Joseph Conrad wondered how one kills fear. God answered that question the night Mary gave birth. You kill fear with trust.

It took great trust for Joseph and Mary to venture to Bethlehem in the ninth month of Mary's pregnancy, or for the shepherds to leave their flocks, or for the Magi to journey so far from home. And it would take trust for you, in your heart of darkness, to turn into your church parking lot some weekday, go inside and let God have a chance at you when the chapel is quiet and you're all alone.

Bethlehem—which literally means "house of bread"—is not just a faraway city; it is as close as your local church. The manger sits in the form of a tabernacle, and your Savior awaits you under the guise of bread. Go to him, close your eyes and hear the angel proclaim, "…Be not afraid; for behold, I bring you good news of a great joy which will come to all the people" (Luke 2:10).

My Father Likes Order

Perhaps, in the final analysis, it is our understanding of God as Father that will help settle our hearts. Consider, for example, the opening of the Nicene Creed: "We believe in God, the Father, the Almighty." Most Catholics, upon reading that first sentence of the Creed, automatically continue with, "maker of heaven and earth."

But do we think about what we're praying? If we were more attentive and less robotic in our prayers, we would read that first sentence as a freestanding truth and not merely the preface to our Creed. I had become so mindless in my approach to the Creed, in fact, that little things like word choice and order didn't any difference make to me. (Yes, I wrote it that way on purpose, to illustrate my point. You see, order does make a difference, and not just on the SATs.)

Note that we proclaim "the Father, the Almighty." But wait, isn't our God almighty, able and willing to destroy our enemies and exalt his faithful above the pagans and heretics? Yes, he is that mighty. So why doesn't it read "the Almighty, the Father?" Why didn't that juxtaposition make the cut with the early Church Fathers when they were wordsmithing the Creed so many centuries ago?

Order tells us a great deal, doesn't it? When ESPN announces a matchup of two sports teams, don't the stars of the teams get mentioned first? When Scripture mentions the Twelve, doesn't Peter always receive primacy from the four Gospel writers, two of whom were themselves part of Jesus' original dirty dozen? Why this particular order? As you may know, the Church was undergoing persecution at the time the early Christian leaders were developing the Creed. In those circumstances, wouldn't the church fathers want to emphasize an all-powerful, lightning-rod-in-hand, ready-to-smite-our-persecutors kind of God?

There is a beautiful lesson in the final order they chose. If we think of God primarily as a judge, our approach to life intensifies. We are more likely to be wrenched with fear. Although we may acknowledge God's presence, we are less likely to invite him in on a daily basis. But if we think of God first as Father, we are more likely to approach him with awe and desire, offering our own life in return for the life he has granted us.

By identifying God first as Father and second as Almighty, the Creed infuses our minds and hearts with a vision of God more consistent with Christ's—as Father, as "Abba" (Mark 14:36). A father's power can be seen not so much in his moments of force as in his moments of peace. A father's hands could be more impressive when he is spanking, but instead he chooses to use them for hugs. A father's voice could be more effective when he shouts, but somehow he finds a more peaceful tone. Would you rather approach God as judge in the courtroom or Father in the living room? Of course, many of us have an image of our own earthly fathers as cold or harsh in comparison to our mothers. Given that, we are often more comfortable with the concept of a judge. We try not to annoy such a dad; we try to make him proud.

What traits do think are most important in an earthly father? Why don't you make a list of them and then rank them in order of their importance. Does the list surprise you? Does the list reflect everything your earthly father is or was, or does it reflect things you feel that he lacked? Does it reflect what you believe your heavenly Father to be? Answer these questions so your prayers won't be rooted in a surface relationship, right down to the Sign of the Cross (for we cannot sign ourselves "in the name of the Father" until we can call him by name).

Practically Speaking

Is God your copilot? Do you let God sit in the car in case you need him, but force him to ride shotgun? Or do you let God into the driver's seat, to steer you through life? The answer to these questions reveals which one you really trust, yourself or God. Pray for greater trust. Total trust in God and in his perfect love drives out fear and, in effect, hands him the keys to your car.

For now, ask yourself what fears are holding you back from God. Do too many questions loom, making it difficult for you to trust your Father? Write out the following questions, leaving space between each to answer.

What will happen when my family members die?

What does my future hold?

What will happen if I don't discern my vocation (or if my kids don't)?

Will I ever get married? Will it last? What will I do to make it last?

What will I do if I lose my job?

What will we do about the problems in our country, world and church?

It's tempting to hold on to our fears because it keeps us from having to trust God more fully. It's easier to say, "I'm afraid" than to say, "I trust you, Lord." He gives us over four thousand promises in Scripture in hope of giving us hope. I've listed several of these promises below.

- Isaiah 41:10
- Proverbs 3:5–6
- Matthew 6:34
- 2 Corinthians 1:10
- Hebrews 12:28

Read through these on your own. Take notes as you read. Get a Bible you can write in. Keep a journal going. Make time for God. If you feel you don't have the time, ask him to free up your schedule.

God commands us to "fear not." If you are living in fear, you will miss the awe-filled opportunity of the moment. Bask in his light and trust it to illuminate your path one step at a time. The shepherds were overcome with fear on the night of Jesus' birth, but their fear soon turned to awe. God can bring the same sense of awe into your life. Put all your fears into the awesome hands of God where "the hopes and fears of all the years meet" and yield peace and trust in him.

CHAPTER THREE

Mass Chaos: A Holy Day of Opportunity

THE FAMILY MINIVAN SITS IN THE CONCRETE DRIVE, a strong hand impatiently thumping the wheel. At thirty-second intervals, the driver scans the fake Rolex on his wrist for the time. Inside the house, it's a melee. A chorus of shrieks fills the hallways: "Where are my pants?" "Is that my shirt?" "Who's serving Mass today?" Our mother—a living saint—furiously patrols the children's rooms like an Army drill sergeant.

My brothers and I push each other into walls on our way out to the garage. Our eyes meet those of our chauffeur, the man who gave us life. He now looks as though he might take it from us. His exasperated expression is a cross between God the Father staring at the apple juice on Adam's chin and Noah on day thirty-nine aboard the ark.

Car doors slam in unison. We start out, enduring the frequent slamming of the brakes at each stop sign, moments that threaten to turn each of the pre-pubescent passengers into living bobble-head dolls.

Tick, tick, tick, tick, seconds fade, minutes stretch, sand falls through the glass. God may be timeless, but the Hart family was not. While our normal weekly experience of the Mass was characterized more by mass confusion than mass appeal, it was our Sunday obligation, and damn it, the Harts were going to fulfill it!

As the family truckster eases us into the parking space, we exit the vehicle. All but two of the family enters the back door of the Lord's house at nine o'clock sharp— doomed to exit at ten o'clock dull. My brother and I, running free from the family unit, dash to the sacristy in just enough time to vest for altar-serving duties. How ironic that we would carry the crucifix, not because of its symbolic importance, but because we, like the Roman soldiers before us, were experts in torture (including, but not limited to, wet willies, wedgies and the always popular sit-on-your-chest-and-pretend-to-spit-on-you maneuver).

The Views From the Pews

An organ blares. The faithful rise. Stragglers enter. Babies cry. Ushers point and cram. Singers miss the note. Children stare blankly at stained glass. Incense fills the air. The masses stand and kneel in unison like some form of Catholic aerobics. Fast-forward twenty years and add cell phones ringing and you have yourself this Sunday's Mass.

An unassuming woman in a florid dress rises to proclaim the living Word of God in a drab monotone, butchering pronunciations of faraway places and long-forgotten people. Some of the faithful strain to listen others begin flipping through the bulletin they grabbed on the way in. It is no longer the Word, but simply words, seemingly outdated and inapplicable to daily lives. When she finishes the reading, the faithful boldly and collectively proclaim, "Thanks be to God."

We now interrupt this flashback for a short newsbreak.

This was my Catholic existence. This was my experience of the Lord's Supper, of liturgy, on a weekly basis growing up. It was an expectation, not an invitation. It was an obligation, not an opportunity. That was my approach. That was my offering of self.

"Honoring the Sabbath" meant, in practical terms, "Don't make God angry." Sit there, pretend to sing and don't you dare try to make your brother, who is serving Mass, laugh. We smelled the incense but didn't comprehend it, noticed the bells but didn't understand them, heard the homilies but didn't apply them. Christian behavior dictated that we not point out how bad the music was, how rude the ushers seemed or how inane the homily sounded.

It was just a battle of time, us versus the clock. And there was no way to win this battle. As a child I could only remain silent and feign interest. This seemed like what most of the adults around me were doing—loving God by fulfilling their obligation, dutifully getting their holy cards punched and keeping their grandparents, watching from heaven, happy.

Some might say that this is a bleak and exaggerated picture. Maybe. Unfortunately, for too many Mass-going Catholics, the average Sunday experience of God is three parts eulogy and one part resuscitation. The liturgy seems to have more to do with death than life, with money than service.

When you were growing up, was your Sunday Mass experience like mine? Worse yet, does this experience sound like last Sunday? If so, what a terrible commentary on "the source and summit" of our faith, as the Second Vatican Council called the liturgy, God's greatest mystery, the pinnacle of our day, week and life.

Was this the sort of worship for which the early Christians so joyfully risked their lives? Was this the experience that had them singing hymns and joy-filled spiritual songs? Was this the intention that our Lord had in the Upper Room when he instituted the Eucharist and called our first bishops, the Apostles, to lovingly enter into the mystery and remembrance of him? What happened to God's day?

Mass Confusion

Sunday has become, not a day of rest, reflection and relaxation, but another day of hard work. It is not a day that we relish but a day that we catch up ("ketchup"—c'mon, that was funny). Cutting the grass instead of cutting out distractions, laundering our clothes instead of laundering our souls, working on ignored homework rather than ignoring work and enjoying our homes. "Honoring the Sabbath" has become a sixteen-hour waking period into which we cram as much stuff as humanly possible in order not to have to do it on top of our incredibly busy weekday schedules. Sunday has less to do with the Son and more to do with the day.

You know how busy you are. Write out a list of all of the things you do on the average Sunday. How many of them draw you closer to God? How much more could your activities turn you toward God?

God established this day of Sabbath rest not because he needs it—he's God, and he's tireless—but because we need it. It is the Sabbath that invites us to the family dinner, beckoning us back to the dining room table, calling us in from the fields of work and helping us to love and enjoy one another's presence. At Mass we become members of the family again; that is how we "re-member" him, as we were encouraged and commanded to do in that Upper Room so many centuries ago.

Unfortunately, we miss the point. Often, we do not see the Mass as a family get-together of the body of Christ. Uninterested worshipers become spectators. The modern liturgy is not as much experienced as it is observed. We are like a family that no longer sits around the dinner table sharing reality but instead sits behind TV trays watching "reality." It's simpler that way, less dangerous.

It's easier to disappear at church than to reach out, easier to pat ourselves on the back for making the trip when others did not. Often, we enter church desiring brevity and anonymity. We want the assurance of salvation but not the strain that comes with transformation. Everybody wants heaven but nobody wants to die.

It is disheartening to realize that the word obligation—as in, it is our obligation to go to Mass—has taken on such a negative connotation. But the truth is, when it comes to Sunday or a holy day of obligation; many of God's children would choose to be anywhere but church. Some of us live not as Roman Catholics but "roamin' Catholics" searching for the quickest Mass, the least challenging homily or the lowest expectation of actual participation.

But, if we would enter into Mass as children coming to the Father's dinner table, we would be enlightened by his Word and fed by his Body and Blood.

What Is This Really About?

Practices and approaches within the liturgy are organic; they change over time. The essence of the Mass, however, does not change. When we open ourselves to deeper levels of understanding, our perspective of the altar is altered. The Mass is no longer just something we attend on Sunday. It's more than a meal and more than a tradition.

The Mass, of course, is a re-presentation and a memorial of Christ's sacrifice on Calvary. Catholics do not believe that Jesus is sacrificed again at every Eucharist but that his one-time historic sacrifice is "made present." In this memorial, "the reality of Jesus' Body and Blood (offered to us at the Last Supper and sacrificed once and for all for us on Calvary) is truly made present in the sacrament under the appearances of bread and wine."[1] In short, Jesus is really and powerfully present to us in his humanity and divinity. We are invited to enter into this mystical reality in every Eucharist: "To receive communion is to receive Christ himself who has offered himself for us" (*Catechism of the Catholic Church* [*CCC*], #1382).

The Eucharist is further understood as covenant, sealing our relationship with God, and as a means to deepen our union with God and one another. It is "'nuptial': Each time we celebrate it, it is a renewal of Christ's total self-gift to us on the cross and our response in love and gratitude as his bride."[2]

The sacrifice of the Mass draws us beyond time and space and cultural constraints. At the liturgy, we all come together in undeserving equality to worship. But this is not the worship of our Old Testament ancestors who worshipped the unseen God in imitation of the angels. No, now we worship Christ in the flesh and unite our sacrifice to his.

The living Word proclaimed in the readings illumines our hearts and minds while the real presence of Christ in the Eucharist leads us to greater perfection and unites us with God and one another. There is a mystical reality here. As the *Catechism* says: "Those who receive the Eucharist are united more closely to Christ. Through it Christ unites them to all the faithful in one body—the Church. Communion renews, strengthens, and deepens this incorporation into the Church, already achieved by Baptism" (*CCC*, #1396).

In the Mass, Christ looks beyond our unworthiness and says, "I love you anyway." Communion is the moment in which heaven kisses earth with the tender lips of hope. As we consume the Lord's Body and Blood, he consumes our souls through the Spirit. This is not a mere spiritual exchange but a physical self-offering of our bodies back "as a living sacrifice" (Romans 12:1).

When it comes to the actual celebration of Mass, how do we offer ourselves back to God in that context? Are we hospitable to those around us? Do we sing, offering something more than a low moan? What tangible physical effort do you make to worship and celebrate the God who enters your presence in priest, community, Word and Eucharist? Open your mind this Sunday to the bigger picture. When you do, wrong notes, long-winded homilies and squalling babies will not consume you nearly as much as the consuming fire of truth and love that exists in Word and sacrament.

Still Haven't Found What I'm Looking for...You, Too?

How many millions of people hit their pillows every night wishing, hoping, praying for true love, selfless love, life-giving love? How many hours, days and months are spent in regret because of love lost? And yet, perfect love exists in the Blessed Sacrament in virtually every city, country and language. The opportunity to love and be loved is present globally.

The world cannot quench our hunger but this eucharistic daily bread can. The words of the self-help gurus cannot lift our spirits or souls the way that the Incarnate Word can. No game of golf or walk in the park will fulfill our need for rest as the Sabbath day does.

Sunday morning ought to feel like Christmas morning, when we want to spring out of bed to see what gifts the loving Father has for his kids. We should be eager to tear into the Mass as we would a Christmas gift—it's the new bike, not the pair of pink pajamas from Grandma. No need to poke and prod and reluctantly open it. The glances at the watch, the scurrying to get ready, the tempers flaring in the car are human responses that should spring only from an uncontrollable desire to be in the presence of our loving Father. The haste to find a pew should flow from an anticipation of the forthcoming miracle, not a desire to be closest to the exit. Our Lord is not obligated to love us. Likewise, we are not obligated to love him back; we are invited to do so.

Extraordinary "Ordinary Time"

We Catholics are obedient. Maybe so few people sing at Mass because it says "refrain" right in the songbooks. Maybe we are taking the term "Ordinary Time" too literally. If anything, we ought to call it extraordinary time as the Creator of all creation comes into our midst; the timeless one enters time, the shapeless one takes on shape in the humblest of forms and actions, so we can know the Father's love.

Of course, we don't often think about it that way, do we? Sometimes we take the simplest things for granted because they are just that, simple. Go to church sometime between Monday and Saturday. Enter into the art and architecture, walk it slowly. Pay attention to the icons, take in the artistry of the statues, study the stained glass. Kneel in the Lord's presence in silence and contemplate the crucifix. Sometimes God's house becomes just that, his house rather than our home.

I have attended thousands of Masses and I usually know the prayers and the readings like the back of my hand. Ask yourself: Do I normally proclaim those prayers without thinking? Do I know the readings like the back of my hand or the front of my heart? Do I stop to meditate upon the incredible sacrifice Jesus made for me on that cross, or do I just dip my fingers in the water and whisk my arms across my chest mechanically? Do I genuflect out of habit or humility? Are my prayers a reaction or a response? Do I take communion or receive our Lord? Do I wait to be blessed and excused with the rest of the children, or do I bolt from the dinner table as if Moses himself were in the vestibule, staff in hand, directing a modern-day Exodus?

The familiar becomes the mundane through repetition. If we dislike the experience we are repeating and are forced to do it anyway, we resent the obligation. If, however, the repetition is illuminating, we will grow to love it and we will be thankful for every opportunity to experience it. Which sounds more like your normal churchgoing experience? How can you change your perspective from one of obligation to one of opportunity?

When the Family Meal Leaves You With Heartburn

A friend once said, "I'll tell you what I hate about the Catholic Mass. The preaching stinks and the music stinks and I get nothing out of it."

I replied, "What I love most about the Catholic Mass is that even if the music or preaching stinks, I still receive Christ." It is never about the peripheral things. They are only the glass and the face of the compass. Christ is the needle pointing us back to God.

The Mass is bigger than the personalities associated with it. If a priest once said something to hurt you, forgive him. If musicians seem to treat the liturgy like a performance rather than a prayer, speak to them humbly and privately in love. If the sound emanating from the choir sounds more like mating cats than the angelic host, join the choir yourself, or sing louder. If the lector's reading style offends you, offer to become a lector yourself.

Opportunity is defined as "a favorable chance or occasion to advance oneself." Simply attending Mass doesn't make you holy. I can sit in a garage all day but it doesn't make me a mechanic. But those who attend Mass daily or weekly have an incredible opportunity to evaluate themselves and become increasingly transformed into God's divine image.

Those who attend Mass occasionally or on holidays should push themselves to see past the struggles, occasional awkwardness or guilt and accept the invitation put before them. God constantly calls us back. He longs to have us seated around his dinner table, as any father would. The invitation others extend to us to join them at the Eucharist is the voice of God. That prompting in the heart is the movement of the Spirit. That stirring in your soul is the response to the quiet call of God within; the sheep know their Shepherd (John 10:27). He calls us not as a group, but individually, by name. He pursues us at every twist and turn. Try to lose him and he won't quit the chase.

Within the Mass, God offers himself as simply and familiarly as he can: through words and actions shared with family and friends over a meal. If you've been far from him, the path back begins with a first step. At every Mass we have an opportunity to encounter God sacramentally, in an intimate relationship. It's the opportunity to have God's living presence within you—how is that for an opportunity, a chance to advance oneself? The opportunity to have sins forgiven and tears wiped away, to have old wounds and emotional scars touched and healed by the nail-scarred hands of mercy and gentleness—these opportunities await us in the Eucharist. In the Mass, we have the opportunity to become more than we ever thought possible and to experience more peace and joy than the human heart can comprehend.

Take on the attitude of those in sacred Scripture who had the opportunity to experience Christ in the flesh. Stop what you are doing, Martha, and enter in as Mary did (Luke 10:38–42). Put aside the nets, leave the plow and step out of the boat; the water is fine. The opportunity to experience God awaits you at a banquet he hopes you'll attend, not because you feel obligated, but because you would never want to miss a chance to be with him and become more like him. The Father wants his family to experience not a piece of the Sabbath, as my family did, but the peace of the Sabbath in all of its fullness.

The Lord did not give us the gift of the church to make us miserable. Christ does not take on flesh in the Eucharist to dwell unnoticed or unappreciated in the corners of our churches. He has come to dwell in us. He is available. Our yearning for him will never outweigh his yearning for us. On Good Friday, Jesus taught us a truth that we dare not forget: God would rather die than live without us. During the eucharistic prayer, when we hear the priest utter the Lord's words, "This is my body given up for you," our response ought to be, "And this is my body given up for you, Lord Jesus." All that we are not, he perfects. All that we are, he accepts, and all that we can be, he anticipates, entering our midst and our bodies to show us the way.

Practically Speaking

Allow me to suggest a few ideas to help you participate in and appreciate the Mass more fully. I've hit upon these after years of trying others that failed.

First, learn a lesson from the military: On time is late, and early is on time. If Mass begins at 9:00 A.M., treat it as though it begins at 8:45 A.M. Wake up earlier, shower earlier, dress the kids earlier, leave the house earlier. If you're saying to yourself, "Hey, it sounds like a nice concept but it's not realistic," ask yourself this: How is it that you can get to the movies in time for the previews but not to Mass in time to calmly find a parking space and a seat, to greet those around you and to prepare yourself prayerfully to enter into the greatest mystery the world has ever known? Do you want to make this a reality? Then ask yourself if the Mass is important enough to merit a change in the schedule and morning rituals.

Second, read the Scripture readings ahead of time. All those names of long-forgotten cities and ancient people aren't nearly as intimidating or difficult if the Mass is not the first time you've heard them. Taking time ahead to pray and think about the Mass readings changes our experience of the Eucharist and our appreciation of God's Word. Try it for a month and see how different the liturgy of the Word— the first half of the Mass—becomes for you and your family. Remember, it is the Word of God, not just words about God. The following week's readings are usually listed in the bulletin but if you cannot find them there, they are available through several publications and periodicals as well as online at sites such as that of the United States Conference of Catholic Bishops (www.usccb.org).

Third, consider the commitments that you've made. The word sacrament literally means "sacred oath." At your baptism and confirmation you entered into a sacramental relationship with God to love him without restraint. Parents who are reading this should bear in mind that you have an enormously important vocation before you: Not only must you bring your kids to church, you must also hand on the deposit of faith. Take seriously the commitments that you made not only to your children, for their spiritual well-being, but also to God who entrusted his children to you.

Fourth, be willing to do the work. Mass was never meant to be entertainment. Read about the Mass. Find out what is happening at each part and its mystical and theological significance. Discover how the Mass relates to daily life. Sit closer to the action. Sing the hymns even if those around you do not. Stay through the final blessing and recessional hymn. Think about those responses you offer. Pray them. Do the work.

Fifth, remain open to change. It is the best thing you can do for yourself and your family. The paschal mystery is all about change. The Holy Spirit is a spirit of change. If you exit Mass unchallenged or as comfortable as when you entered, odds are that you missed something. Allow the power of God to render you speechless and the mercy of God to render you free from pride. Offer your body back to him in his house so that when you are sent back out of his house, you are prepared in body and spirit for what lies ahead.

CHAPTER FOUR

Body Building: Tearing Down Our Temples

THE QUICKEST WAY TO IMPROVE THE SELF-ESTEEM OF everyone in America would be to hire professional photographers to work at the Department of Motor Vehicles. Better yet, we should be allowed to supply our own license photos, that one picture from home in which we actually look good. Every driver's license in the country would display a shot of a confident, well-dressed specimen on a good hair day. Then drivers' licenses would no longer function merely as visual proof of identification or assurance of the ability to operate a motor vehicle. Oh, no. Your license would function as proof that at one point in time you were thinner, younger, tanner, taller, lighter or had more hair.

Aren't we funny when it comes to appearance? Think about the daily rituals we undertake. Men apply chemicals to mask their natural body odors then take razors to their faces and finally tie silk nooses around their necks. The poor woman is forced to pluck and shave, scorch, flatten and curl, all before perusing a closet filled with "nothing to wear" and cramming her feet into uncomfortable shoes. It's a lie to say that women are more concerned than men about appearance. It's just easier for men to get dressed (possibly because of the lack of hair).

Regardless of what we may claim, on some level everyone is image-conscious. That doesn't make us evil; it proves us human. Appearance matters in modern society. That's why we spend millions on the latest infomercial product designed to attack fat in just minutes without any sweat on our part. That's why billboards advertising beer or fast food never show guys with beer guts or girls with love handles. We want to fit in (to the dress) not stick out (of our shirts).

Have you ever called friends to see what they were wearing before you got dressed for a party? Have you ever returned clothes because they looked better in a dressing room than at home in your bedroom? Do you ever wear vertical stripes or black because they make you look slimmer? Have you ever tanned your body for a wedding, gone to the gym right before a date or starved yourself before a dance? Sure you have; I have, too. But why do we do those things? There is a certain minimum expectation, isn't there? And when it's broken, we hope we're not the one breaking it.

Why do we spend so much time making the exterior of our temples so attractive, while the interior is vacant and in need of serious renovation, even demolition? How do we have time to go to the gym but not to the church? Why are we more concerned with what we don't eat (diet) than what we do (Eucharist)? Our priorities dictate our practices. As Jesus said: "...where your treasure is, there will your heart be also" (Matthew 6:21). And most of our hearts are most moved by the desire to look good when we're being looked at.

The Slim Gym

The scene is familiar. Smell the overchlorinated pool. See the aerobic machines in need of a wipedown. Listen as a muscular toothpick in sweats talks you into securing a second mortgage so you can "get fit." Never mind that it's direct deposit and never mind that you'll hardly show up over the next twelve months.

Deltoids flail, biceps burn, triceps tear. And over there in the corner, men who believe a well-toned body is the ultimate prize and women who believe they can change any body-sculpting madman into a sensitive mate exchange glances, nutrition tips and, occasionally, phone numbers. It's the last bastion of the singles scene that doesn't involve a computer, a semi-formal dance, a bar or a blind date set up through mutual friends. It's the gym.

Exercising often becomes a process that needs exorcising. What happens at the gym is a version of what happens on campuses, in offices and at parties across the country. Eyes scan the workout floor not only for possible mates but for the body types they find most appealing. Men and women deconstruct the opposite sex into body parts, judging potential love interests according to exterior appearance. This kind of shallow observation knows no gender bias. It drives reality television and provides gossip fodder over lattes.

In these settings, habits are formed and unhealthy standards established. If we were to be honest, the flirting that takes place is in fact scoping, leering, ogling, dismantling, objectifying, comparing and lusting. Bodies become tools for temporary gratification. The result? Dysfunction and dating frustration.

Our perspective of the human body and the body's purpose is skewed. We need to change our perspective and reevaluate ourselves and our bodies in relation to the body of Christ.

How do we encounter Christ in the flesh in the everyday places beyond the parish walls? Sure, we might be going to church and offering God our bodies for an hour a week, as we discussed in the last chapter, but what about the other 167 hours? What do we see when we peer into the mirror? What do we look for in the bodies around us?

Who Is Responsible? You. Me.

Somehow, we are never thin enough or alluring enough. As a culture, we are steeped in what we are not. Here are some of the personal demons unleashed by the monster of vanity: self-hatred, pride, ego, lust, judgment, self-doubt, jealousy, greed, emptiness, loneliness. The list goes on and on.

We've been so inundated by images of an oversexed culture of "thin and sleek" that we have lost a sense of the sacredness of the body, the temple of the Holy Spirit. We desperately search in all the wrong places for the inner peace and love that only God can offer.

A particularly troubling modern failing is the tendency to scrutinize God's creation with such a critical eye that we fail to see the unique beauty in our perceived "flaws." This is one reason I imagine God looks sadly on the gyms, bars, clubs and similar places where young adults gather. Not because the buildings themselves are intrinsically evil but because the spirit behind them, masked as recreation, is indeed a form of re-creation—distorting reality to meet a false, ungodly standard of who men and women are and what the nature of the human body is.

Poor self-image often gives way to self-hatred. Where does this overarching need to "fit the right image" come from? The disturbing truth is that we have become so desensitized to the reality of the human body that even a gorgeous body is no longer good enough. Pick up any magazine cover and see if you can find a wrinkle. A pockmark. Flab. Those covers are not reality; they are air-brushed virtual reality. Reality isn't good enough.

As we "set straight" the perceived flaws in God's design, we see eating disorders become rampant, breast implants become commonplace, binge drinking become acceptable and sexual promiscuity become the norm. We ignore or repair all that makes us unique and enhance whatever makes us common.

As a culture, we are steeped in image, embroiled in our humanity, devoid of all recollection that we were created in the image and likeness of the Divine. Scripture reminds us that "all is vanity" (Ecclesiastes 1:2). The more we feed this monster of vanity, the more it consumes us.

Of course, ours is not the first culture to struggle with a misunderstanding of the truth about the human body. Ancient Corinth, for example, was a large and cosmopolitan city in Greece. It was a seaport town and a trading center and so, like any city then or now, it had its share of sexual immorality. Having visited there, Saint Paul knew its temptations and struggles well. The words he wrote to the Corinthians a few years after his stay there still resonate today:

> Do you not know that your bodies are members of Christ? Shall I therefore take the members of Christ and make them members of a prostitute? Never! Do you not know that he who joins himself to a prostitute becomes one body with her? For, as it is written, "The two shall become one."...Shun immorality. Every other sin which a man commits is outside the body; but the immoral man sins against his own body. Do you not know that *your body is a temple of the Holy Spirit* within you, which you have from God? You are not your own; you were bought with a price. So glorify God in your body. (1 Corinthians 6:15–16, 18–20; emphasis mine)

Paul knew well that being a Christian, a child of God, meant more than just proclaiming who Jesus was. Even the devil could do that (Matthew 8:28–31). Paul knew what true love was and he knew that love was, indeed, about flesh—the sacrifice of it.

Words vs. Action

In his Gospel, Saint John gives us a fascinating picture of Pontius Pilate as he struggled to extricate himself from responsibility for the biggest sacrifice of all time. Pilate knew the power of words. He countered the false words of the religious leaders who accused Christ. He understood that the words of the crowd had the power to free or to condemn. He knew his words to the guards could bring scourging and crucifixion. He knew the word from Rome was to keep peace at all costs. He exchanged terse words with Jesus about the nature of truth.

Pilate was restless as he wrestled with his decision. He knew the locals and the pilgrims would judge his judgment. He resorted, finally, to the written word. He had an inscription placed on the cross above Jesus' head. In Hebrew, Latin and Greek the sign read, "Jesus of Nazareth, the King of the Jews" (John 19:19). Here was the Son of God. He put God's will before his own in bodily sacrifice, in action. He laid it all on the line—for you and for me.

His sacrifice forces me to ask myself the difficult question: To whom do I belong? Am I my own? Do my body and life proclaim that I belong to God, or to the world? If I say I am my own, then I belong to myself, free and clear, although that means I deny the role of the Creator, the Author of my life. If I am my own, I can do what I want as long as I am a good person. Jesus Christ is not my Lord, and I do not need a Savior.

However, if I proclaim that God is my God and I belong to him, does my bodily temple proclaim Christ's lordship? Do I invite him in or leave him on the steps outside? Do I proclaim my Catholic Christianity with words but deny that reality by the way I use my body? Is Jesus' call to purity consistent with my lifestyle?

Tough questions often lead to uncomfortable answers.

Author, Author

If I do accept that God is the author of life, do I see my life as a story that God is writing, or do I think of God as someone in my story? Too often, sadly, I used to view God as a mere character that I included in the play of my life, not as the Creator who "writes souls" into being through his providential pen and who loves people into existence through their parents. Tom Sawyer, you know, could not write lines for Mark Twain, and Macbeth did not write soliloquies for Shakespeare.

Where do my talents and beauty, internal and external, come from? Who breathed life into whom here? When it comes to your life, God is the ultimate authority on the subject. Don't stifle his highly creative process. Let him keep writing and your life will be a page-turner. If you accept that God is your "author," people will know his book by your cover, so to speak, by your inner spirit radiating through your physical appearance.

God is a God of details. Every detail about you, every talent, every physical attribute has a purpose. What is special about you? Look in a mirror. Do you see God in the freckles, the wrinkles, the acne or the other "imperfections"? Love is in the details. Look around. Who are the people that God has brought into your life? Who has influenced your identity for the better, drawing you closer to your God? Who has pulled you away? Your environment influences your identity. Is your environment a place where people encounter God? Where has God been present in your life?

Body Language

Without words, our bodies speak volumes about Christ. We proclaim Jesus, the Word, silently in our flesh, in our dress, posture, openness and attitude. Your body makes a statement about your relationship to God in the same way a wedding ring, Roman collar or religious habit do. We shouldn't overthink how we dress, but we should consider more carefully what we communicate about our beliefs and motivations through our dress.

You will have to shatter the misconceptions you have developed about you and your dream mate. That includes radically redefining what your core values are and what you are looking for in a partner. Think about what you are and are not willing to sacrifice. Admit and reconcile the fact that physical desires sometimes sidetrack your spiritual needs. Decide what you are going to do about this. Identify those demons that exist deep within your heart, soul and sexuality and exorcise them. Ask God for the courage to eliminate them.

Campuses, gyms and bars are filled with empty teens and twenty- and thirty-somethings because too many young adults focus on a self they don't like, separated like orphans from a God they don't really know. They know how they want to be seen. They know how they don't want to end up. They know with whom they don't want to end up. Beyond that, it's a crapshoot.

But the story your body tells should never be dictated by who is "reading" it. Remember who your Author is.

By taking on the limitations of the flesh through the Incarnation, Jesus propelled the dignity of flesh to a whole new level. He expects much only after having given much. Jesus is a model of self-mastery and self-sacrifice. His vocation demanded total obedience and discipline. The word *disciple* comes from the same root word as *discipline*. We cannot be students or followers of Christ if we are unwilling to control our appetites, especially our physical appetites, through self-discipline.

Time to Exorcise

From the divine perspective, the overweight, beleaguered guy on the treadmill, trying desperately to take control of his body, is more beautiful than the chiseled Adonis curling weights in a vain attempt to become more attractive to women. Correct? Honestly, we don't know either of their rapidly beating hearts. We make a judgment as to their motivations based only on their outward appearances.

Instead, we can choose to put on Christ (Galatians 3:27) and see through his eyes that the bodies he created are sacred temples, not buildings to be dismantled. We can make godly choices regarding not only how we present ourselves but also what our motivations are when we look at others.

Each of us is unique. Every time we judge another, every time we look in the mirror at one of those "details" of God's design and sigh with disenchantment, we belittle the artist's finest work. The devil has won.

When we see not as the world sees but as God sees, however, our view of ourselves and others breaks off the suffocating grip of conformity. No longer do we renew our gym membership so we can look a certain way for others;

we work out to keep our temple a healthy dwelling place for the Spirit.

Practically Speaking

Scripture tells us to "put to death" the deeds of the body that we might live in the Spirit (Romans 8:13). The Church affirms spiritual exercises that help us to stay right with God so that our souls rather than our bodies lead us. Fasting is one such grace-filled exercise. When we fast we do more than deny ourselves food; we make a conscious effort to offer our bodies to Christ. We offer our hunger to God and in that offering there is grace.

Similarly, working out takes on a new purpose when we keep Christ in mind. Don't just go for a run but offer up your run for a specific intention. Say, "There may be other things I'd rather be doing, Lord, but I'm going to offer up this run for _____". Pray for the person or intention as you run. That sacrifice will change your perspective on the exercise and hold you accountable in the process.

Manual labor is another great way to get back to the basics. Clean out that garage. Plant the flowers you've been meaning to plant. Attack that closet you are afraid to open out of fear of falling objects. And while you're in that closet, ask some tough questions about certain outfits. Make tough decisions to get rid of anything that might send the wrong message. Glorify God with your bodily temple and inspire others to glorify him—not you—when they see you walk by.

Take the time to affirm others, especially children, for traits that have nothing to do with appearance. Affirm somebody verbally at least once a day, whether someone you know or the stranger who hands you your coffee. Take advantage of all of those moments to recognize and acknowledge those who serve you—the waitress at lunch, the delivery guy at work, the crossing guard at school, the postal worker or the bagger at your local grocery.

The more we notice our tendency to value the external over the internal, the more easily we will be able to shift our perspective and learn to value the things that really matter.

CHAPTER FIVE

Reconciling Your Issues: Thinking Inside the Box

YOU KNOW HOW IT IS. WE GIVE THE "DRY CLEAN ONLY" tag on the new shirt more attention than the "may cause cancer" warning on cigarettes. We dismiss the command to wear sunscreen until we have to get a mole checked. We ignore the admonition to drink more water until we form that first kidney stone. The date on the milk carton means more to us than the warning on the beer bottle. Clearly, our obedience is dictated by the immediacy, not the severity, of the consequences.

I'm guilty of breaking more rules than I can count, and most likely you are, too. We tend to approach rules with the attitude that knowing them makes it easier to bend them. We act like this in our faith, too, living as if God only sees what we let him see. Handled this way, our experience of the "rules" can dictate not only our approach to life but also our progression toward death. But the Catholic church has a means of dealing with our inclination to bend, break or otherwise mangle the rules of life and our relationship with God: the sacrament of reconciliation.

First Things First

When it came to rules, my parochial school experience was rooted in one thing: disobedience. The goal of my parochial education, of course, was supposed to be exactly the opposite: obedience. It didn't matter if I comprehended why I was going to confession, as long as I went. "It's what good Catholics do," I was told.

Well then, why don't good Catholics just stop sinning? I thought to myself. Of course, I never actually uttered that outright. I had learned to keep such thoughts to myself by third grade following the fiasco of the "I spit because Jesus spit, Sister" incident. (See John 9:6 for my rationale.)

I vividly recall my first confession. I was petrified. My palms were drenched with sweat. My shirt collar felt like a noose. My fidgeting and pacing caused my school uniform Toughskin pants to sound like hissing cats. As I slowly crept forward in the line, the vision of the alternating red and green lights with each vanishing sinner and departing saint left my mouth dry and my mind blank. How heinous a sin could this poor ten-year-old have committed that such torture should be required?

I entered the confessional and heard the heavy Gaelic drawl of the old Irish priest. He spoke so fast I could barely understand him so I spoke fast in reply. There was no remorse, no regret, no true understanding of the sacrament— just a beleaguered expression of pre-adolescent guilt overshadowed by obvious fear and anxiety. I gave three quarts of perspiration and five uninteresting sins. He gave me three Our Fathers.

I left the confessional happy to be alive. The padded

wood kneeler creaked as I put it down to recite my penance. The sweat subsided. Something had just happened; I was sure of it. I just wasn't sure what it was. I had approached God in some way. I had thought about Jesus, sort of. My body made it through unscathed but my soul had some catching up to do.

I already knew the Ten Commandments inside out: They functioned less as a moral compass and more as a means to determine how a particular action measured up against the threat of eternal damnation. My pubescent Catholic life was becoming a search for the loopholes instead of the Lord.

That "justification" theology was my biggest downfall as I hit the teenage years. What behavior could I justify that would still allow me to squeak through the pearly gates? I wanted a faith where I could have as much sex as I wanted, smoke and drink as much as I wanted and be as completely self-absorbed as I wanted. I found it. It was the religion of Me. We had one member, we were totally broke and we were destined for hell.

The God I knew from confession was unapproachable, so I looked inward instead of upward. Over time I learned that the rules aren't made to be broken—I was. You are, too. Our approach to wholeness in Christ has to begin with brokenness within.

Thou Shalt Not

My image of God the Father, enthroned in heaven in flowing white robes and Birkenstock sandals, was overshadowed by my certainty that he didn't want me to have any fun. Not only was God all about rules; he'd drop anybody that strayed off his path. Parochial school should have taught me how to live, but instead I learned how not to die and burn. The result was that I treated Moses' Commandments with the same reverence I reserved for one of Letterman's "Top Ten" lists.

So, my moral life was an exercise in hell avoidance. I feigned contrition with a halfhearted sincerity in hope that, should I die tonight, God would go easy on me. I knew how to say I was sorry for breaking the rules. I promised to stop doing the things I had just confessed even though I had no intention of doing so. I even knew my Act of Contrition. I apologized to God without knowing why my sins were sins. (As to that, years later as a married man I learned something about true contrition, namely, if you're going to apologize, you had better know what you are apologizing for or else you'll find yourself in even more trouble.)

For several years I saw confession as apologizing to a priest who "stood in" for God. If anyone had corrected this impression in religious education class, I missed it because I never listened. Later, I learned that it isn't merely a priest to whom I am confessing, but truly, it is Christ. During reconciliation, the priest sits in *persona Cristi capitas*—in the person of Christ the Head. He offers not his mercy but that of Christ.

Later, also, I would come to understand the difference between apology and repentance and between the private and public nature of sin. In repentance you don't merely turn away from something; you turn toward something else (see Acts 26:20). And my sin, no matter how private it is, has a ripple effect on those around me.

Everyone in my life suffers to some degree from my selfishness and sin; no sin is ever completely private since we are all bound together in one mystical body. The world looks down upon it as weakness, but as I matured, I came to see the beauty involved in humbling yourself and going before another, staring into the eyes of mercy and admitting failure.

For years, my faulty understanding stymied my approach to Christ, keeping me from the greatest gift that God had to offer: total forgiveness. I totally failed to connect the dots given me in Catholic school and at countless Sunday Masses. It was only when sin and misery reached such a blinding level that I earnestly began to seek not fame or fortune but the peace that only Jesus can give that my approach to Christ began to change. I learned that Saint Augustine was right when he said that we are all restless until we rest in the Lord.

SurMOUNTable Goals

In order to change a skewed understanding of the sacrament, it helps to realize Jesus came not to abolish the law, but to complete it (Matthew 5:17). He came to show us how to "...have life, and have it abundantly" (John 10:10).

I was not unique in my confusion. Many people today dismiss the moral code set forth in the Ten Commandments because they assume that religion is all about rules, conformity and some sort of guiltridden mind control. The doctrines of Christ, safeguarded by the Catholic Church, are dismissed as contrary to human freedom. In this context, obedience is seen as a form of weakness. By extension, that would make Jesus Christ the weakest man to ever walk the planet.

The question Catholic teens ask me most frequently in regard to sexuality is, "How far is too far?" What's behind that question? What young people are really asking, once we look beneath the euphemistic wordplay is, "What exactly is everything I can do sexually—without going to hell?" They want to clearly delineate the line so they can approach it and tap-dance on it and then justify their behavior.

Can we mature in our understanding of the Law so that we mature in our approach to Christ and our readiness to receive God's mercy? Well, let's take a minute to look at it more closely:

The Law (Commandments)	The Life in Christ (Fulfillment)
Thou shalt not:	*Thou shalt:*
...have other gods before me.	...be single-hearted toward me.
...take the Lord's name in vain.	...be reverent in speech and conduct.
...dishonor the Sabbath day.	...keep priorities.
...dishonor thy father and mother.	...be respectful and obedient.
...kill.	...defend life, womb to tomb.
...commit adultery.	...be faithful to vocation, future spouse.
...steal.	...be trustworthy.
...bear false witness.	...be honest in word and deed.
...covet thy neighbor's wife (lust).	...have only pure admiration.
...covet thy neighbor's material goods.	...be grateful for what you possess.

Do you get it? Living a faith-filled life is not so much about what we shouldn't do as about what we are called to do as we move forward in God's love. You can use the parallels on the previous page as the beginning of your examination of conscience the next time you prepare for the sacrament of reconciliation. In particular, ask yourself how you measure up to the list on the right as you prepare your soul for the sacramental mercy of Christ.

Love Thy Neighbor

Turning away from sin does not mean shutting ourselves off from sinners entirely; it means refusing to frequent environments or hang around in tempting situations that will lead us to sin lest we become mastered by it once again. Jesus is calling us to live in the world, but not be of the world (John 15:19).

Modern Christians are not called to create a separate subculture but to permeate modern culture. We use an earth-shocking humility and unapologetic gospel example as our greatest weapons. We are not meant to cloister together with our "Lord's latte" from our Christian coffeehouse, sucking on our "Testa-mints," shopping only at our church gift shops, condemning all but our Christian radio stations, allowing only cars with fish symbols to cut in front of us in traffic.

Christianity is not an exclusive privilege for the masses at Mass; it is a necessary invitation to the sinners at the mall, at the office, in the classroom and the locker room, on the cul-de-sac and even in our own household.

Making It Real

As we saw in the first chapter, Christianity is not about merely being a good person but about becoming a new person in Jesus Christ. "And he died for all, that those who live might live no longer for themselves but for him.... Therefore, if any one is in Christ, he is a new creation; the old has passed away, behold the new has come" (2 Corinthians 5:15, 17).

So how do we become that new person, clear our "record" and get straight with Jesus? I'm still a sinner. Sometimes, I still get a little apprehensive when I go to confession and I don't know the priest or can't look him in the eye. Aside from airplane bathrooms, the confessional is the only place where I feel claustrophobic.

What is it about confession that can be so overwhelming emotionally? For me, it was the fact that for too many years it was confession alone, without reconciliation. In my pride, I used to justify my lack of self-control saying the situation was too difficult and that's why I sinned. Sure, I acknowledged my sin but I rarely claimed it. I would blame temptation on the influence of others, and I would avoid taking the blame myself.

I wanted God to see me in the right light, so I tried to show him what I was doing well, all that was right in my life. Out of shame, I kept the brokenness, emptiness and sin hidden away. I was like the child afraid to show his report card to his father. In a sense, I was comparing my "grades" with those of my peers and deciding that I looked pretty good in comparison. In effect, I measured my growth in holiness by other people's growth. God wanted me to be reconciled to him and to grow in his plan for my life.

The Reality of Sin

The word *forbidden* adds a naughty ring to any conversation or suggestion. Forbidden sin can be especially attractive to those who are out to prove their independence and individuality.

Conveniently, we often forget that sin carries a consequence. Saint Paul doesn't mince words: "For the wages [result] of sin is death..." (Romans 6:23). We just don't get it. We find it difficult to believe that a life in Christ, following his commandments, will be half as much fun as our life near Christ—where we can still be in control.

Determined to go our own way, we push Jesus out of the driver's seat and take the wheel. Sometimes we don't even let him ride shotgun. In fact, the more grievous the sin, the worse seat we end up assigning to our Savior. Venial sins get him a place in the car. Mortal sin locks him in the trunk or abandons him on the side of the road as we speed off toward "life" in the name of "fun."

Our need for control stems from our lack of trust in God. We don't like the idea that God might lead us somewhere we don't want to go, and we can't believe that he knows what he's doing with our lives. We approach Jesus with one foot on the gas pedal and the other planted on the ground. Our body drags our soul behind it. We falsely believe that our independence is only as great as our ability to pick and choose what rules we obey.

Some of us end up as moral relativists believing that my truth equals the truth. In fact, much of our country today is trapped in the falsehoods of moral relativism, which claims that man is the center of the universe and that there is no absolute truth. (If there is no absolute truth, by the way, there can be no judgment, heaven or hell, and everything Jesus said is a lie. The ramifications when you take the next "relatively" comfortable step are mind-boggling. Yet morally relative arguments prevail throughout our culture on newscasts, in political debate, on blogs and so on.)

Relativism is so much a part of the culture that it doesn't even stick out anymore. A comment like "there is no right answer" is easier to stomach than the real answer: "life is tough" or the better answer, "tough is good" or the best yet (and completely honest), "sometimes life just sucks."

Maybe we don't want to hear the truth about suffering. People who can put a probe on Mars, clone animals and solve the intimacy issues of eighty-year-olds want to alleviate all mystery and end all pain. They forget that they have no scientific explanation for why we have an appendix in our gut, pay our actors and athletes more than we do our teachers and police officers, and celebrate labor by taking the day off work.

The reality is that life is filled with sin and suffering and there are two kinds of people: those who run from it and those who deal with it. Do yourself a favor and learn to deal with it. Memorize Blessed Charles de Foucald's Prayer of Abandonment and pray it daily:[1]

> Father, I abandon myself into your hands; do with me what you will.
> Whatever you may do, I thank you: I am ready for all, I accept all.

> Let only your will be done in me, and in all your crea-
> tures.
> I wish no more than this, O Lord.
> Into your hands I commend my soul; I offer it to you with
> all the love of my heart,
> for I love you, Lord, and so need to give myself, to sur-
> render myself into your hands,
> without reserve, and with boundless confidence, for you
> are my Father.

Love is truth and truth can hurt. The truth for too many of us is that we soften the message of Christ, replacing a heavy, splintered cross with a light, smooth, shiny one. We've been taught that Jesus is merciful, and too often we confuse mercy with ambivalence. Our approach to the faith is one of convenience. We don't want to hear that missing Mass or that premarital sex are sins. We take black-and-white issues and claim that they are gray.

For example, instead of admitting the fact that abortion is homicide, some play the "what if" game, throwing out scenario after scenario, each with a more difficult storyline, hoping that if a chink can be made in the impenetrable logic of life then the whole debate will be rendered senseless. We read about abortion in the paper but classify it as a political debate. How is the child's life in the womb worth less a few months or pounds or grams earlier?

Reality scares us, so we hide under the blanket of God's love and pull the covers up high over our eyes, hoping our heavenly Father will think it's cute. We concentrate on the "loves the sinner" part of the famous equation, dismissing the very necessary prefix, "God hates the sin."

There are black-and-white issues in this world, and they can be hard to take. When the truth is inconvenient, we label the Bible as "outdated" and declare the Church to be "archaic." People say, "I don't support abortion, but I won't tell another person what to believe" or "I won't tell my friend that sex outside of marriage is wrong," which sounds nothing like what my Lord tells me: "...[I]f your brother sins, rebuke him, and if he repents, forgive him" (Luke 17:3).

Does this stuff ring true? Does it sound an alarm in your conscience? What should be done about it? What should you do about it?

The Reality of Mercy

Too often, our relationship with God becomes one of a lazy employee and a short-fused boss. "Don't get caught and you won't get in trouble."

God does love you, the sinner. He promises that "...he will wipe away every tear...[and will] make all things new" (Revelation 21:4–5) and that "...[T]hough your sins are like scarlet, they shall be as white as snow" (Isaiah 1:18). The only sin he can't forgive is the sin for which you don't ask forgiveness.

The truth is that the only thing keeping me from living sainthood is myself. The same is true for you. Christ is waiting to free you from yourself, and he is willing to do it at your local parish, through the words of your friend, your parish priest. This is Catholicism in its purest form, rooted in surrender and obedience.

This sort of humility gives us a faith that still has tread

on the tires when the rubber meets the road on Wednesday and the songs from church on Sunday are no longer on our lips. This sort of humility renders us vulnerable to Jesus' unyielding pursuit of us, sinners that we are.

To be holy or "set apart" does not mean that we are set apart from Christ as sinners, but that we are set apart from sin for holiness. He brings love behind doors that no one will open. He embraces the unembraceable. He saves souls. He changes lives because he brings mercy and forgiveness. He didn't come to abolish the law or to strike sinners repeatedly over the head with it, but rather to perfect it, to kiss the intrigued and repentant sinner's brow with it.

It's amazing how quickly we sinful humans can lose sight of our own sin. It's even more amazing how we can allow fear of God to keep us from his mercy and the fullness of life. His promises are clear but we ignore them. We hear them at Mass but we don't really listen. But right here, right now, you can have a newfound appreciation for and hope in God's healing power in the sacrament of reconciliation. Jesus wants you to turn from sin, because when you actively turn from sin you turn toward him.

Jesus Christ is waiting for you. He is not afraid of your mess. He is bigger than your sin. Confession focuses on the sin; reconciliation focuses on the sinner. The Commandments are not the antidote to suffering or the golden ticket through the pearly gates. They are like X rays, enlightening those areas within that need to change.

Christ is the surgeon waiting to reconstruct those broken areas of your life, those areas you attempt to ignore or hide. Jesus is calling you—pick up the phone. Better yet, schedule an appointment and swing by his office.

Practically Speaking

Reconciliation is like exercise: There will always be an excuse not to go, so you just have to get up and do it. If you don't have a regular confessor, a priest whom you know and trust and can visit frequently for the sacrament, find one. Schedule reconciliation. Go every few weeks, even if you aren't sure you need to. Have others hold you accountable.

As with hitting the gym, the more you go the more you will begin to see noticeable benefits in your joy, confidence and overall outlook on life and family. Grace is a powerful gift, though it's not so much a steroid as it is a vitamin! You won't see the effects of grace as much as you will be sustained by grace. You will see your soul begin to lead your flesh in moments of weakness instead of the other way around.

Take the time to develop a testimony or story about the grace that God has shown you through frequenting the sacrament. Refine that testimony. Practice it and then share it. Maybe you can offer your testimony to a confirmation or RCIA class at your local parish and help put other people's minds and hearts at ease. Help dismantle the misconceptions regarding the sacrament, and give someone else the gift of mercy that you yourself have received.

CHAPTER SIX

Recreational Sex: Living in the Flesh

U P-UP-DOWN-DOWN-LEFT-RIGHT-LEFT-RIGHT-B-A. That was it. That was the secret. That was the code that kept me from accomplishing anything productive for two semesters in college. My obsession had started much earlier, though, back when video game controllers still only had one "fire" button. Atari held me captive.

I loved the old Atari video games when I was growing up, so much so that my older brothers used to call me "the vidiot." Eventually, though, "Pong," "Asteroids," "Space Invaders" and even "Pac-Man" failed to challenge me. Technology progressed, Nintendo arrived and my intellect tried to catch up as we evolved from "Donkey Kong" to games with actual men, men who had guns.

My academic career during college took a brief detour each afternoon as my roommates and I took turns braving the mercenary-filled jungles in the popular game "Contra."

Simply by entering a magic code you received 99 lives each, allowing even the least skilled player to advance through the preliminary and advanced fields. Everyone had a shot at beating the game.

How many hours did I sit in our dorm room on that $20 couch from Goodwill as most of higher education, dozens of intriguing conversations and countless mysterious women passed me by? But hey, I finished the game. The secret code offered me something that "Pong," "Pac-Man" and "Donkey Kong" never could: the ability to reign supreme, beat death and never hit the reset button.

My wasted hours, however, led me to a sad conclusion. Specifically what were video games created for? Recreation. And what did they accomplish? Ignoring God's creation.

Sitting for countless hours in front of that television did little for my salvation and little for my God. That's not to say that video games are a total waste of time or intrinsically evil. Positive things can come out of them and they can be harmless fun. They can, however, shape our expectations about life and how we should experience it.

Virtual Reality

The video game world can trick us into thinking that life should be like the world of virtual reality. Life is a whole lot easier in the gaming world. There, we are all-powerful. Our actions hold few, if any, consequences, and we can start over as often as we want to.

Other forms of technology also change our perspective, causing us to feel more powerful and invincible than we are. We see it not only in video games but also on the

Internet, in the world of genetic engineering, through artificial contraception and so on. The temptation is to play God. It makes me think of another game, a certain game of hide-and-seek in a garden (Genesis 3:8).

While the story of the Garden of Eden is not necessarily meant to be read as scientific truth, reading it opens our eyes to a simple fact: Human beings want to create their own reality, and the temptation to do so was there from the start. Adam and Eve wanted a world in which they were in control, so they disobeyed God. When that backfired they tried to hide from him.

But God had a better plan, sort of like a video game in that it includes a "reset" option. First God gave us creation, then Adam and Eve brought us the Fall and then God responded with redemption. The "reset"? Redemption includes the call to repentance through which God forgives and restores us again and again.

The chance to reset through repentance and reconciliation is not a given, however; it is a gift. And unlike life in the video game world, the actions that lead us to hit reset do have real-life consequences. It's a mistake to think that we have countless "lives" or that self-help books or inner-focusing rituals can help us push the reset button and pick up where we left off, unchanged.

This is particularly true in regard to sexuality. God certainly forgives us when we repent for using our sexuality in ways he never intended, but we can't always undo what we've done. The reset button won't bring back your virginity, or your baby lost through abortion, or full health to someone suffering from sexually transmitted diseases such as herpes or HIV. If we follow God's game plan from the start, however, and make every effort to let the Spirit of God guide us, we won't have to worry about reset in this area.

If you have lost your virginity and you want to start over, recommit to chastity. If Christ came back today, he wouldn't separate the sheep from the goats (see Matthew 25:31–46) by sending "virgins to the right, non-virgins to the left" but according to who is and is not living chastity.

The Flesh May Be Weak, But the Spirit Is Willing

Crash diets don't work. If a woman loves donuts or a man loves buffalo wings, they have the choice: control their flesh or schedule the angioplasty. Simply eliminating the temptation isn't enough; the body must be retrained and self-control must come into play. The same is true in the battle for purity.

You are a sexual being. Everyone is. Your body was created with sexual desires for a reason, a purpose. However, the fact that you were created with such desires doesn't mean they should dictate your life. Sex, in and of itself, is not the goal of life. It should not be the motivating factor. Sex is not a mere act. Sex is not power.

Sex is a language, gifted to us by God, that speaks of commitment and self-sacrifice. Sex is an expression of unconditional love, a unifying experience for a man and woman who have offered their lives to one another and to God.

Sex outside of the bonds (that's right, the bonds) of holy matrimony is contrary to God's will for several reasons.

Sex is procreative; it is the means through which God

brings a child into the world. At its most fundamental level, that is what sex is all about. As the church teaches, every child must be brought into the world through an act of love on the part of the parents. In this, conception models God's own creative nature. God forbids us from conceiving a child in any other way—through any artificial means of conception.

Sex is also unitive; it is a binding act that unites not just the bodies but the hearts and spirits of the couple to one another and to God. Sex creates a permanent bond of love meant to foster the unity of the couple. That unity helps create an environment congenial to the raising of children. Premarital sex is sex without permanent commitment and nearly always opposed to the creation of a child.

In marriage, the couple confirms their openness to motherhood and fatherhood, and the purpose of the sexual act is fully realized. In Catholic wedding vows, the man and woman declare that they will willingly and joyfully accept children. In achieving this end, artificial contraception is not an option, although a couple may space their children using the method commonly known as natural family planning.

The couple also states that they will remain together as long as they both shall live. This permanent commitment transcends the graying, wrinkling, sagging and slowing down that come with time. This vow affirms that the attraction shared between husband and wife exists beyond the borders of sexual satisfaction: "No matter what happens," the couple is saying to each other, "you are more than a body, and sex is more than an act. I am in this forever."

If you are sexually active and not married to your partner, reconsider the language that you are using. It's God's
language, and it is not open to adaptation or interpretation
to suit your situation.

Anti-Sex or Anti-Selfish?

Many people think that the Catholic church is anti-sex.
Nothing could be further from the truth. The church is pro-
commitment and anti-selfish. Throughout his pontificate,
the late Pope John Paul II wrote and spoke extensively
about the nature of the person and human sexuality. In fact,
from 1979 to 1984 he devoted 129 Wednesday audiences to
the subject, and these addresses collectively are known as
the theology of the body.

The theology of the body provides a comprehensive
view of the human person encompassing body, soul and
spirit and delving into anthropology, history, eschatology
(the destiny of humanity), celibacy, chastity and sexuality.
The pope tackled issues such as the meaning of the human
body in its maleness and femaleness, what marriage reveals
about the nature of God himself, the meaning of chastity, of
love, what God had in mind from the beginning when he
created humanity and more.

This teaching, still largely unknown among Catholics, is
life-changing, a gift of the Spirit to the twenty-first century.
There are plenty of books available to help you understand
this magnificent work, such as: *Men and Women Are From
Eden: A Study Guide to John Paul II's Theology of the Body*
by Mary Healy (Servant Books) or *Theology of the Body for
Beginners* by Christopher West (Ascension Press).

As Mary Healy says in *Men and Women Are From Eden*: "[T]he theology of the body...is God's wonderful providence for our time. This is in part because the old arguments for the church's moral teaching simply were not adequate to meet the challenges of the third millennium. It is not that they were false; they simply were not convincing enough for people living in a dramatically changed social context."[1]

The social context has indeed changed, but the church continues to safeguard human dignity by refusing to condone the manipulation of God's precious gift of sexuality for selfish gratification. Contraception, premarital sex, the attitude that "sex is fine as long as you are in love" all lead to a false sense of freedom.

We don't find true joy by surrendering to our passions; this provides only temporary gratification. True joy consists in the proper exercise of our freedom. As Archbishop Fulton Sheen said, "The root of all our trouble is that freedom for God and in God has been interpreted as freedom from God. Freedom is ours to give away. Each of us reveals what we believe to be the purpose of life by the way we use that freedom."[2]

What's the Use?

Sex in contemporary society is primarily about use (pleasure) rather than purpose (unity, procreation, pleasure). Where has this left us as a society?

Decimated. Pornography ensnares both men and women, and families suffer. Divorces proliferate, leaving millions of young people leery of entering marriage themselves when they grow up. Sexually transmitted diseases leave innumerable women unable to bear children. Mothers are left to raise children alone, and women are abandoned as they age because their men used a "forever" language with a "for now" intention. Countless men and women are embittered after having been thrown aside when they have fulfilled their "use."

Consider this: When singles hook up or married people stray, sex is usually the goal, although we can fool ourselves about it, and often do. But what usually happens after the sexual thrill fades? Heartbreak and shattered lives. This should tell us something, but it doesn't seem to. Too many people leave one illicit sexual situation and fall right into another.

When sex becomes the goal, it has lost something intrinsic—its spirit of self-sacrifice, of total and permanent commitment. In other words, it loses all that makes it sacred. When it is separated from its God-designed purpose, it becomes an act of using someone—or using oneself in the act of masturbation. And let's be truthful: Politicians might argue that oral sex is not actual sex, but anyone who is honest knows that's ridiculous.

If you are a young adult who wants to avoid the heartbreak that ultimately accompanies premarital sex, choose chastity now. The self-control, spirit of self-sacrifice and understanding of love that you acquire will also help to protect you from divorce when you do marry. Chastity now and a right understanding of the nature of love and commitment will help give you the inner strength to make it through the difficult times that come in all marriages.

What are we offering and taking, giving and using? If we want to advance to that next level of life, men and women need to take a look at it all. Otherwise, the "game" is over. Of course, if sex were just a game there would be no consequence, no emptiness, no pain and no sin.

Caught in the Mousetrap

The temptation of masturbation always comes up when you talk about a healthy view of sex. There is nothing new about it. Nor is masturbation primarily a guy's sin. It has, however, received new life, new emphasis, in this culture of death. And one of the most terrible aspects of masturbation is that it is often coupled with pornography.

Pornography is a demon that emotionally, psychologically and spiritually suffocates men and women. Before the Internet, a boy had to have a friend with access to his dad's secret stash of *Playboy* to see pictures of naked women. Pre-teens would have to loiter outside a convenience store until an evil-minded, "empowering" adult would agree to head inside and buy them porn.

Today, porn is only a click away. Young women take seductive photographs of themselves, put them on Web sites and ask strangers to rate them on their "hotness". We are drowning in a sea of selfish men and denigrated women. Our culture is so sexually skewed that it hastens its own descent into depravity by suggesting that moms and dads encourage masturbation, equip kids with birth control and watch pornography themselves to keep the marital spark alive.

Studies suggest that a large percentage of women who are involved in pornography were abused as children or young adults. The cycle of abuse feeds itself. They may find work at strip clubs or appear in explicit videos. An already lowered sense of self-esteem plummets to new depths as they accept the lie that they are unworthy of a deeper love or are only valued by society for their looks, their body, their "liberated" sexuality or their willingness to compromise it.

If what I'm saying strikes you as simplistic or prudish, I urge you to stop right now and pray. In your prayer, ask Jesus himself to give you his perspective on modern sexuality. Then sit in silence. Is he prompting you to guide your mouse to the porn site so that you can discover his perspective? Does he suggest that you call a sex line? No.

If you struggle with an addiction to pornography or masturbation, seek out a mature Christian friend of the same sex, a confidant or confidante, and ask him or her to hold you accountable to chastity in this area. Give the friend permission to challenge you frequently, to berate you as necessary, to affirm you often and to call you to holiness daily. Ask the Blessed Virgin Mary and Saint Joseph, the perfect models of chastity, to join their prayers to yours and help you remain chaste.

Boys Will Stay Boys...if Allowed
As I speak at high schools and universities across the country, I'm consistently amazed both by the extent of the modern sexual struggle and the fact that the answers are so obvious but so often ignored.

The most common question I hear from women is,

"Where are all the good guys?" That's ironic, because the guys always ask me, "Why do girls always date guys who treat them poorly?" You know I'm not talking about issues like stalking and violence that must, of course, be dealt with forcefully and legally. But too many women have lowered the bar. They date men who have little interest in them beyond their bodies. So are the women more at fault? Absolutely not. This is a two-way street. Far too many men are all too willing to take advantage of women however they can.

Women who begin to fear loneliness and desire companionship sometimes get caught in a trap. They want a healthy, wholesome relationship but, fearing that they will never find a great guy, they slowly lower their standards. On the altar of fear they sacrifice virtues they once considered mandatory in a prospective partner.

Men quickly accept such a sacrifice and offer "love"—attention—in return for sex. Sometimes these men—self-absorbed, intent on pleasure—go on to abuse women verbally, emotionally and even physically. Still, women offer their most precious physical gifts, their sexuality and dignity, in hopes of a lasting love. Even if they find a relationship, they are forever altered. Too many women are left, in time, with nothing more than shattered hopes, a reflection they'd rather not look at in the mirror and doubts that anything better can exist.

When the Pursued Get Chaste

Consider, for a moment, a different type of couple: a man who exercises self-control in his dating relationships and a woman who holds out for only such a man. Refusing to ever allow their bodies to lead their souls, they take to heart the words of Scripture: "...[F]or God did not give us a spirit of timidity but a spirit of power and love and self-control" (2 Timothy 1:7). They put God first, each other second and their own "needs" a very distant third.

Can it be done? To live chastely as single young adults in the twenty-first century is difficult, but very possible. Coworkers may mock them and friends may misunderstand them and hardly anyone will believe them, but early in courtship, from the very first date, they will have set their plan: to guard and honor chastity. In short, they are guarding their salvation.

They pledge to mutually protect their own chastity and the chastity of the other. They walk this narrow road together, finding room for three on the path and inviting Jesus himself along not as a spectator or a scorekeeper, but as the one who will lead the way.

Ask yourself these questions: If you are still single, do you live by a pledge of chastity? Are you willing to make such a pledge? Are you willing to share it with the person you are dating, right from the start? Even married couples are called to live chastely, using sex as God has ordained. Are you willing to live chastely in marriage? If the answer to any of these questions is no, then figure out why. What is holding you back?

Your Mission Possible: A Virtuous Reality

Living chastely, in or out of college, is as difficult as any mission a young adult will ever undertake. Chastity is more than abstinence. The *Catechism of the Catholic Church* gives us wonderful insight:

> Chastity includes an *apprenticeship in self-mastery* which is a training in human freedom. The alternative is clear: either man governs his passions and finds peace, or he lets himself be dominated by them and becomes unhappy [cf. *Sir* 1:22]. "Man's dignity therefore requires him to act out of conscious and free choice, as moved and drawn in a personal way from within, and not by blind impulses in himself or by mere external constraint. Man gains such dignity when, ridding himself of all slavery to the passions, he presses forward to his goal by freely choosing what is good and, by his diligence and skill, effectively secures for himself the means suited to this end" [*GS* 17]. (*CCC*, #2339)

A man who would rather die defending his wife's salvation is a man after Christ's own heart. Where Adam failed to defend and protect his wife in the Garden—Eden—our Savior succeeds in the Garden—Gethsemane—offering his life for us, his bride, the church (Ephesians 5:25).

A woman who would rather die than compromise the salvation of her husband is a woman after Mary's, the New Eve's, own heart. When a couple stands before a priest of God, in the house of God, before an altar of sacrifice, and they genuinely pledge their lives to God and each other, they understand the sacrament beyond the ceremony. They offer each other far more than "legal" sex on their marriage bed; they pledge their very selves.

The wedding day is far greater than the tux and the gown, the groomsmen with bloodshot eyes, the bridesmaids in dresses they won't admit they hate or the upcoming honeymoon in Hawaii. It is the offering of two lives—body and soul—in complete and total selflessness. He pledges that her soul is primary, in sickness and in health, in good times and in bad. She, too, swears to such an oath. He loves her enough to deny his own urges. She thinks enough of him to deny hers. The result: a man and woman who are far from perfect but close to God.

Brothers, this is the life you are called to when you claim Christ as your Lord. What are you looking for when you head out at night? What traits are you most drawn to in women? Your eyes reveal your heart and your words show your motivation.

Women of God, what does this mean for you? Among other things, it means you will have a man who won't cheat on you when he takes a business trip. You will have a husband who will adore every inch of that expanding tummy in the first trimester and every strand of uncombed hair in the third. You will have a spouse who knows what it means to die to himself, a man after Christ's own heart. You will have the man you noticed and made time for because you weren't wasting your time on the low bar or singles' bar guys.

Brothers and sisters, how do you find such a person in the modern scene? Pray hard and keep the standards high. Review the places you go. Ponder the things you wear. Look deep within yourself and decide what you want to offer to others—your sexuality or God's gift of chastity?

If this kind of purity sounds out of reach to you, your body is leading your soul. If you have suffered abandonment, abuse or other wounds in past relationships or within your family, don't allow your hopes to be dashed by the burdens of the past. What is the deepest longing of your heart? Contemplate the words of the late Pope John Paul the Great:

> It is Jesus that you seek when you dream of happiness; he is waiting for you when nothing else you find satisfies you; he is the beauty to which you are so attracted; it is he who provokes you with that thirst for fullness that will not let you settle for compromise; it is he who urges you to shed the masks of a false life; it is he who reads in your hearts your most genuine choices, the choices that others try to stifle. It is Jesus who stirs in you the desire to do something great with your lives, the will to follow an ideal, the refusal to allow yourselves to be grounded down by mediocrity, the courage to commit yourselves humbly and patiently to improving yourselves and society.[3]

All of us are God's handiwork, and we were created with a purpose. Jesus Christ changes our perspective of our sexuality by changing the way we view our purpose, which is not to seek pleasure but to bring life.

Practically Speaking

Living with chastity is a difficult call in a world obsessed with sex and devoid of healthy affection. Take strength from the fact that many others, in every vocation, are living it successfully and joyfully. Take hope from sacred Scriptures. Meditate on the following verses:

> So shun youthful passions and aim at righteousness, faith, love, and peace, along with those who call upon the Lord from a pure heart. (2 Timothy 2:22)

> For this is the will of God, your sanctification: that you abstain from immorality.... For God has not called us for uncleanness, but in holiness. (1 Thessalonians 4:3, 7)

> But if Christ is in you, although your bodies are dead because of sin, your spirits are alive because of righteousness. (Romans 8:10)

> I appeal to you therefore, brethren, by the mercies of God, to present your bodies as a living sacrifice, holy and acceptable to God, which is your spiritual worship. (Romans 12:1)

> Do you not know that your body is a temple of the Holy Spirit within you, which you have from God? (1 Corinthians 6:19)

> Do not be mismated with unbelievers. For what partnership have righteousness and iniquity? Or what fellowship has light with darkness? (2 Corinthians 6:14)

> ...[A]nd put on the new nature, created after the likeness of God in true righteousness and holiness. (Ephesians 4:24)

> Blessed are those who hunger and thirst for righteousness, for they shall be satisfied.... Blessed are those who are persecuted for righteousness' sake, for theirs is the kingdom of heaven." (Matthew 5:6, 10)

If you are currently dating, ask yourself: "Is this person leading me closer to or further away from Jesus Christ?" If the answer is "away," stop and think. Consider if your joy and soul are worth this. Be willing to bypass the for-now partner in favor of waiting for the forever partner. If you are married or feel called to the vocation of marriage, write out a sort of mission statement for yourself and your present or future spouse. List your goals and objectives for the marriage and what you consider to be the most important traits in a healthy, God-centered relationship.

Once you submit your understanding of sex to Christ, once you invite the Holy Spirit into your bodily temple and let God's truth enlighten you, you'll find your soul leading your body more often.

CHAPTER SEVEN

Finding Courage in Suffering: Blood, Sweat and Tears

I T'S SATURDAY NIGHT, AND THE EMPTY CASE FOR THE RENTED movie sits atop the player. The last lamp has been turned off. The smell of burned popcorn still fills the house as a result of a first attempt gone horribly wrong. The only light in the room emanates from the glowing box ten feet from the couch. The same fifteen-second audio loop from the movie has been playing for twenty minutes because the DVD menu screen popped up just as the popcorn fiasco began.

Then the movie begins accompanied by a brooding, creepy musical arrangement. The hero and heroine are introduced, along with a cast of utterly forgettable and soon-to-be-butchered extras. The "nice trip to the cabin" or "after-hours party at the college" quickly takes a turn for the worse. You jump when a quick cut reveals a corpse

95

drenched in blood. But this is just a movie, so everything is OK—right?

At that moment, there's a horrendous noise in the dark kitchen. Your oversensitive nerves are shot. "What's that??" you yelp.

"It's the icemaker," replies your companion. "It goes off every thirty minutes. Has since 1982."

Sheepishly, you turn back to the movie just in time to see another extra get obliterated. For unknown reasons you continue to watch. Finally, the homicidal madman (who clearly was not hugged enough as a child) is grotesquely massacred. You're left with an empty popcorn bowl, a racing heart and violent mental images that you must now reconcile as you double-check the door locks, make sure the dog is out back and proceed to your bedroom for a good night's sleep.

Yeah, right. Even your bedroom isn't safe now. The closed doors harbor threats. You view the windows for their escape-route potential. It's easy to be brave when the movie is playing, you're on the couch and the nameless extra is scurrying around after a killer; you're not the one in real danger. It's when the movie is over and everyone else is asleep that your bravery is tested. The "brave" thing is to go investigate, but what is your heart telling you? What is keeping you in that bed? What force now has your heart racing even faster than it was during the movie? It was easy to control the situation when you were the spectator, but now you're in the scene and you have a choice to make. Will you be the extra or the hero? The answer rests not in your head, but in your heart.

Bravado Revisited

Courage comes from two Latin words: *cor*, which means "heart," and *ragio*, which means "to act." In essence, courage means "willing to act from your heart." Whereas bravery means "unafraid" and is to a great extent mental, courage is entirely heart-led. By definition, if you are afraid, you are not brave. But if, even while afraid, you act from your heart, you are still courageous. Courage is not the absence of fear; it is the refusal to be mastered by it.

Courage is a *charism*, a gift of the Holy Spirit. Since it involves a denial of self, it is hard. But hardship and difficulty can be good because they challenge us; when we respond with courage, tough situations build character.

To develop character, we need enough courage to face hard tests without running away. In order to do that, we desperately need God's perspective. What is your heart bent on this day? If you were to abandon all else and truly act from your heart, what motivations would be guiding your moral decisions? It's easy to cast judgment on priests or politicians or celebrities and dismiss them as sinners or people who don't live up to their calling. Meanwhile we, the unnamed masses, "bravely" hide from the moral dilemmas and truths in our own homes, schools and jobs. When have you been courageous in your faith this year? In what ways have you personally answered the call to act from your heart?

If you're going to move forward in your faith and move on in courage, first you must be humble enough to realize what factors are forming you and who, or what, might be lord of your heart rather than God. If Jesus meant what he said—"For where your treasure is, there will your heart be also" (Matthew 6:21)—then before you act, you might want to take a quick look around to make sure your heart is where it ought to be. You need to know this Jesus you are going to follow. How do you know him? Where do you get your image of God, besides your family, Sunday Mass, parochial school, cable TV and your own brain?

Focus, Focus

"Perspective" is an interesting word. It stems from the Latin root words of *per* (through) and *specere* (to look). So, quite literally, having perspective means being able to "look through" a situation. It means that you are able to remove yourself from your own preconceived notions long enough to see the bigger picture, the world that exists beyond your own immediate surroundings.

Scripture is meant to broaden our perspective, to help us look through history (His-story) and see our own story hidden in the lives of brothers and sisters portrayed in its pages. On first glance, Advent is about the birth of the baby Jesus. With broader perspective, however, we see it is as much about Jesus' Second Coming as it is about his birth. Our perspective allows us to celebrate Good Friday because we know what happened on Easter Sunday. When we read the story of the storm at sea in Matthew 14, we see Simon Peter as an unfaithful failure because he only took a few steps on the water before he doubted and began to sink. A changed perspective, though, shows him to be the courageous and faithful apostle to whom Jesus would later entrust his church on earth. No one else got out of the boat.

No one else took that leap of faith. Those three steps that Peter took were three more than the rest of the clan. It's all about perspective.

How divine that the same eyes which welled with joyful tears one starry night in Bethlehem also shed the broken tears of a widowed mother holding the same blessed body years later. The only thing separating the Nativity from the Pietà is time and perspective. The wooden manger lay in the shadow of a wooden cross. Joseph held and wiped the blood off his new baby boy that night in Bethlehem, and Joseph of Arimathea would share a similar honor three decades later.

Biblical scholars affirm that it was not a barn, but a cave hewn out of rock that served as the first Christmas tabernacle, which is a perfect mirror image to the Easter tabernacle of the rock-hewn tomb. It was out of a cave that the Word became flesh and out of a cave that the Word breathed life once again. Both caves acted as a starting point for heaven, although both were "ending points" in the eyes of earth.

Extra, Extra, Read All About 'Em!

I didn't read the Bible growing up. The truth is, aside from Sunday Mass, holy days, weddings and the occasional greeting card or crossword puzzle, I was never really exposed to Holy Scripture. As I became friends with other Christians of all denominations, I was often amazed at their command of God's Word. I also felt somewhat cheated by my own church for leaving me so ignorant of the Word of God.

Joshua, Rahab, Gideon, Deborah, Josiah, Esther, Jairus, Zacchaeus, Mary (wife of Clopas)...all names I had heard, sure, but they were just names. These characters in history meant little to me, and the same is probably true for you. Then there are the other characters in the story, the "extras." The Bible doesn't even give their names: Naaman's servant girl, the woman at the well, the man born blind, the woman with a hemorrhage, the boy with five loaves and two fish. The extras in the Bible make brief appearances and disappear. What role do these people play in this huge ethereal storybook, and what am I supposed to learn from them? What difference does it make to me how many loaves this kid had or how many husbands the woman at the well had gone through?

What it comes down to is perspective: They were not extras and you are not an extra, either. There are no extras. In the mind and heart of God, you are in the Garden of Eden, faced with the choice of trusting God or submitting to sin. You are among the olive trees in Gethsemane, staring evil in the eye, deciding whether to choose death to self, which will bring life, or preservation of self, which will ultimately bring death.

But everything we've talked about so far—making that shift from cradle Catholic into postmodern, relevant, Jesus-loving Catholic Christian—actually involves much more than a change in perspective. Change takes faith, abandonment and courage. The perspective shift is mental. The next shift is far more difficult because it requires action, and that's where courage, the willingness to act from the heart, comes into play.

My favorite scene in the film *Braveheart* depicts Mel Gibson (Wallace) rallying his countrymen on the plains of Stirling, admonishing them to fight for their freedom. When Wallace poses the question, "Will you fight?" one nameless extra retorts, "No, we will run and we will live." The ensuing speech transforms their fearful hearts into courageous hearts. The heavily outnumbered, undertrained army of farmers rabidly took to the battlefield, knowing that the blood about to be spilled would very likely be their own. A close look at the extras in that scene always gets my adrenaline going. Maybe it's a guy thing, I don't know, but when the extras armed only with pitchforks begin shaking their farm tools and screaming at the opposing army like madmen, it really pumps me up. We don't see that kind of courageous passion anymore.

Isn't that the same kind of passion that Christ showed for us with his life and in his final eighteen hours on earth? Isn't that the same kind of passion that all Christians, regardless of denomination, are called to live out still today? It's a total abandonment of self and a complete renunciation of everything that renders our hearts blind, numb or fearful. Why do we fear anything with God on our side (Romans 8:31)? We need to heed the rallying cry of our Lord and follow his command: "Do not fear." (In the gospels, Jesus tells us not to fear more than he tells us to love!) Our hearts, if bent on him and directed toward him, will lead us back to him.

Kiddie Pool or High Dive?

Remember, God doesn't call the equipped, he equips the called. If you believe in God but are not willing to take action about your lifestyle, then you are not letting Jesus be your Savior. You cannot believe the gospel and still live your life the way you want. Maybe you are so desperately afraid of the un-fun lifestyle you think God will give you that you'd rather wade in the kiddie pool of life than take a run off the high dive. But regardless of what changes it means for you, Jesus Christ is bigger than anything.

For example, he's bigger than suffering. When our lives are full of pain, when everything is blood, sweat and tears, whenever we feel abandoned and left to suffer, we have to turn to God. Not partially, not halfway, but completely and totally. When the waves come and the sharks circle, God isn't one option; he is the only option. At times like that, we need to remember what Saint James penned, "Draw near to God and he will draw near to you" (James 4:8). God is alive. He is active. He is closer than you think. Through an act of your will, turn to him and you will not be disappointed.

When we give God control, he reaches out to us just as Jesus reached out to Simon Peter as he began to sink after his steps on the sea. His Holy Spirit is just one prayer, one movement of our heart away. Christianity is not about immediate gratification; it is about immediate grace. Christ is a Savior, not a Santa; a God of faithful fulfillment, not an ATM of "quick change."

"Draw near to God and he will draw near to you" (James 4:8). This verse is beautiful in its simplicity; it's a great one to know by heart. The next time the storms of life come your way, trust in this promise. It will change your perspective in the midst of suffering.

Womb to Tomb

You were delivered physically on your birthday and spiritually at your baptism, but what's been going on since then? Is Christ calling you to something more in your life this day? Picture your bedroom. Every morning before your first foot hits the floor, you have a decision to make. Whose are you today? Those who follow Christ make that decision for him daily. They know that he can turn the darkest circumstance into light and life.

It's like the garden tomb. Jesus' tomb was a place of transformation. Once opened, the tomb allowed the sunlight in and the Son's light out. That's how it is with our hearts when God breathes life into us. Nevertheless, for many of us our hearts remain the tomb of Holy Saturday instead of the tomb of Easter Sunday. As suffering comes and goes, so does our trust. We become hardened by the world. Our hearts of stone refuse to allow the light in or out.

Is your heart the tomb of Holy Saturday? Is there a self-created stone rolled before the entrance? If so, push back the boulder. Break down the walls. Have the courage to invite Christ to truly take control of your life. Open your tomb today, and if you need help moving the rock, ask for it.

Practically Speaking

Sometimes, you just need space. Space, though, is a tricky thing in some families. Those of you with "imposing" families (there's a gentle euphemism) may be made to feel that personal time or privacy are somehow "rude" or uncaring or unfamilylike. That's not healthy. It's essential to communicate but being made to feel that you have to communicate every single thing you are feeling, regardless of where you are in the pondering process, isn't helpful. Your prayers should not have to be a family bulletin on your current condition. Everyone needs some space, so don't feel guilty about that.

Sometimes you just need time. God commands us to take a Sabbath. Maybe if you actually made your day of rest a day of rest, things would be different. You'd have a better outlook on life. You would be more patient, more aware of other people and more trusting about God being in control. Speaking from experience, Sundays are the greatest gift God has given me in the course of the week. I never knew how great they were until I actually began making Sunday about God and my family and not about me and my work. Keep the Sabbath holy (set apart), and your life will be blessed in ways too numerous to mention.

Finally, open yourself up to the Holy Spirit. Invite the Spirit to move within you and to change your perspective toward life and suffering, to give you the courage to respond in faith. The Bible reminds us that the Holy Spirit leads us to truth (John 16:13), helps us to avoid sin (1 Corinthians 6:11) and gives us unparalleled understanding of the mind and heart of Jesus (1 Corinthians 2:6-14).

Tap into the Spirit's power more fully, fan the flame of the sacraments of baptism and confirmation that stir within you and watch as not only your vision but also your approach to Catholicism become more focused and active. Let your tomb become a womb for his dazzling new life.

CHAPTER EIGHT

Student Counsel: More Than a Popularity Contest

I T'S AMAZING HOW LITTLE I RETAINED FROM MY PAROCHIAL school experience. I remember random things like the name of my half-blind bus driver, the toddler-friendly height of urinals, the aura of power of the crossing guard's bright orange sash, and the nun who taught me how painful sarcasm could be.

When it came to actual knowledge regarding the faith, however, I had the retentive capacity of concrete. Ask me to name the Brady kids, no problem; ask me to name the twelve apostles, we're in trouble. Ask me where we kept the candles in the sacristy, I'm your (altar) boy; ask me why we held candles next to the priest as he read the Gospel and you're out of luck. I knew when I was supposed to go to confession but not why. I knew why I was supposed to read the Bible but not how. I knew how I was supposed to follow God—obey the rules—but not where.

My quest for truth, limited as it was, ended in confusion. I was a student in need of counsel, wearing plaid in a world of gray. I had a lot to learn, and I still do.

I ask myself, which is more difficult: aging or maturing? Time is the only irreplaceable commodity in life. Money can be replaced. Jobs can be replaced. Material possessions can be replaced. Time is slippery, uncontrollable, a treasure not to be wasted.

When you're young, you live for Saturday; it means all play and no work. When you're older, Saturday is mostly work and little play as you run errands and clean the house. When you're young, you can't wait to get out of school. When you're older, you wish you could get out of work and go back to school. When you're young, you'll do anything to stay up and avoid going to bed. When you're older, you can't stay up and you long for bed.

When you're young, you do what you're told. When you're older, you do the telling but not so much the listening. This can lead some folks to think they know more than they do, an especially dangerous attitude when what they think they know isn't actual knowledge at all. For example, when you ask a cradle Catholic with this mind-set a question about the faith, you might get a shaky reply backed up with the vague statement, "I've been Catholic all my life." End of conversation.

But what do we really know as Catholics? Not enough.

Assuredly, parochial schools, religious education programs and youth ministry are not entirely to blame for our ignorance. These are supposed to support *catechesis*, the handing on of the faith that should take place first and foremost at home. Unfortunately, most of us did not receive our primary catechesis at home. Sure, we may have had pious parents or grandparents with personal devotions to the rosary or prayer. Yes, many of our relatives made it to Mass with disciplined regularity and served in various ministries with consistent dependability. When it came to really passing on the faith at home—teaching truths and not just saying grace before meal or bedtime prayers—most Catholic families fell short. And not enough of us are inclined to fill in the gaps by attending religious education classes or reading books about the faith as adults.

The Age of (Needing a) Reason: Generations X and Y

Where has this widespread ignorance of the faith left us? Ask a range of Catholics about the meaning of Advent, the Church's teaching regarding the Blessed Mother, why contraception is sinful, what the Church's pastoral response to homosexuality is, why the Church regards the sacrament of penance as a communal celebration and so on. Too often you'll be met with a blank stare or a hesitant answer.

Young people, especially, lacking any systematic understanding of Catholic faith and doctrine easily fall prey to an "enlightened" worldview that emphasizes personal fulfillment or stresses the equality of all religions or urges them to search out their inner "gods." True theology plays second fiddle to personal philosophy. We try to make sense of our adolescent "formation" and end up being merely culturally Catholic.

In effect, we grow old in our faith but we don't grow up. We mature physically and socially but not spiritually. In our teens, twenties, even our forties and fifties we might retain the instinct to pray right before bed or before meals but we can neglect to come before the Lord in any meaningful way in the course of the day.

Rather than remaining childlike, as Christ commands us in telling us to receive the kingdom of God "...like a child" (Mark 10:15), we grow up childish. We pray before bed, often half asleep, but fail to set ourselves before God in prayer when we wake up, get ready for the day, head off to school or work, sit in traffic, take a break, shop, stand in line and all the other realities of daily life. Jesus calls us to "...turn and become like children" (Matthew 18:3) so that we will stay close to him—open, dependent, willing, humble and wide-eyed—not so that we fail to mature.

Why don't we invite Christ into our day more often? If you simply don't think of it, then Jesus is still distant, not yet a friend or brother. Yet he identifies himself as brother and friend in the gospels. Ask yourself if you have a friendship with Christ or an acquaintanceship.

What's the Difference?
A friend comes over and helps you strip wallpaper off the bedroom wall in your starter home. An acquaintance offers to lend you a steamer. A friend hops in the car and heads for the airport when your ride falls through and you're stranded at the curb with a pile of luggage. An acquaintance answers your call and asks, "Whoa, what are you gonna do?" A friend offers you his savings when he hears your loved one is sick and your insurance might not cover it. An acquaintance goes into a monologue about the inefficiencies of the health care system. A friend cares enough not to

order one more beer even though he might like one, because you've had too much. An acquaintance urges you to drink more because it will make for a funny story. In short, a friend is willing to sacrifice for you: "Greater love has no man than this, that a man lay down his life for his friends" (John 15:13).

It's vital, however, that in our relationship with Jesus we don't confuse friendship with equality. A proper understanding of our relationship to God, the creator and sustainer of life, is essential. Jesus invited even the most hardhearted and egregious of sinners to receive him. And when they did, their actions acknowledged his authority.

Zacchaeus the tax collector repaid those he had defrauded four times as much (Luke 19:8). The blind beggar received his sight and "...followed [Jesus], glorifying God" (Luke 18:43). When Jesus invited Matthew the tax collector to "Follow me," Matthew got up and followed him (Matthew 9:9). Jesus' friendship was evident but so was his lordship. Christians who approach Jesus merely as a buddy are missing the boat.

This is what a friend can do that an acquaintance cannot: call you out of your sin and selfishness for your own good. You still love friends like this no matter how much it hurts.

Discipleship 101: The One Elective Needed to Pass

Why am I stressing the friendship and the lordship of Christ? Because if we are his friends then we are also called to be something else: his disciples. A disciple is a student, one who sits at the feet of a teacher in humility, openness and readiness for instruction.

To be a Catholic means to embrace discipleship and all that such a demanding identity entails. As the *Catechism of the Catholic Church* says: "From the beginning, Jesus associated his disciples with his own life, revealed the mystery of the Kingdom to them, and gave them a share in his mission, joy and sufferings" [cf. *Mk.* 1:16–20; 3:13–19; *Mt* 13:10–17; *Lk* 10:17–20; 22:28–30] (*CCC*, #787).

The Gospels paint quite a picture of Jesus' band of followers from the meek to the overzealous, the proud to the humble, the cowardly to the courageous. I imagine that during his three years of public ministry, Jesus put them through something of a spiritual boot camp—or sandal camp, if you will. His words and manner toward them and their response to him give us a perspective on what it means to be a true disciple, a student who learns, a Christian.

The following are some Scripture passages that reveal what a disciple of Christ should look like. Use these for prayer and meditation, asking the Lord to help you as you try to become more like him.

- Being a disciple means becoming smaller: "So the last will be first, and the first last" (Matthew 20:16).
- It means being a servant: "[L]et the greatest among you become as the youngest, and the leader as one who serves" (Luke 22:26).
- It means that Christ takes precedence in our lives: "He must increase, but I must decrease" (John 3:30).
- A disciple follows the guidance of the Holy Spirit: "When the Spirit of truth comes, he will guide you into all the truth" (John 16:13).

- A disciple is willing to die to self or even die for the faith: "If any man would come after me, let him deny himself and take up his cross and follow me. For whoever would save his life will lose it; and whoever loses his life for my sake and the gospel's will save it" (Mark 8:34–35).
- If we want to follow Christ we must be eager to share the faith with others: "...Go into all the world and preach the gospel to the whole creation" (Mark 16:15).
- A disciple bridles the tongue even when that is difficult: "If any one thinks he is religious, and does not bridle his tongue but deceives his heart, this man's religion is vain" (James 1:26).
- A true follower of Christ speaks words that are affirming and constructive: "Let no evil talk come out of your mouths, but only such as is good for edifying..." (Ephesians 4:29).
- A disciple controls the flesh: "...[I]f you live according to the flesh you will die, but if by the Spirit you put to death the deeds of the body you will live" (Romans 8:13).

There is much more that Scripture shows us regarding what it means to be a disciple of Christ. When you have the time, get out your Bible and look up some of those additional passages. You will learn that as a disciple you should carefully discern what sources and forces form you (see 2 Timothy 4: 3) and put the needs and lives of others before your own (see Romans 14:13-16). At times you might feel persecuted, broken, ignored, threatened and even hated because of Jesus Christ (see 2 Corinthians 4:9; 2 Corinthians 11:24–28; Matthew 22:5; Acts 4:29; John 15:18).

True discipleship means that you avoid immorality, pray unceasingly, are open to the gifts of the Spirit and that you realize that you are part of the larger mystical body of Christ (see 1 Corinthians 12:12, 27; 1 Thessalonians 4:3; 1 Thessalonians 5:17; 1 Corinthians 12:4–11).

Discipleship is an invitation to flee from darkness in order to walk only in the light. It means moving away from environments and activities that are inconsistent with the way of life offered by the Holy Spirit. This way of life is demanding, but holiness demands sacrifice and love demands effort.

Ready or Not, He's Got a Plan

You never want to stop learning in life. You might choose not to learn, but that is your choice and an unfortunate one. People never actually say that they are finished learning, they just close themselves in such a way that it is evident. John Paul the Great held World Youth Days not to speak to the youth but, as he put it, to listen to them. He never stopped learning; that is a characteristic of a true disciple. The world's greatest modern missionary and potential future saint never forgot he was a student first.

God wants to use you; he has plans for you. He's ready to call on those talents and gifts and skills that he's bestowed on you. If you're consumed with what you're not when you look in the mirror, remember that God sees all that you are. He sees your promise and he sees his glory within you. He's not checking to see if you measure up to the person next to you on the chart of potential; he's interested in how you're using the potential he's placed within you. He'll bat down every excuse you throw at him to ignore or refuse his gifts.

Throughout Scripture, God calls and uses different types of people with different types of issues. Sometimes he called people who were down on themselves because they were focused on their own sin. Sometimes—rather often— he chose people who were low on the social ladder or even outcasts. Plenty of these people could easily have claimed an excuse for not serving when God called. I once read a list once that went something like this:

> Jacob was a liar. David was an adulterer. Abraham was too old. Timothy had ulcers. Peter was a coward. Moses was a stuttering murderer. Mark was undependable. Hosea married a prostitute. Naomi was widowed, as was Ruth. Jonah was disobedient. Miriam was a gossip. Thomas doubted. Elijah suffered from depression. Paul was a murderer, too. John the Baptist dressed funny. Martha was a worrywart. Zacchaeus was very short. Mary was only a teenager. Lazarus was dead.[1]

So, what's your excuse? God sees something in you, something you might not even see in yourself. He's calling you to stay humble, dependent and aware of your need for him so that you are better able to serve him.

No need for a second pair of sandals. Don't worry about the second tunic. Jesus, not the mall, will supply you with everything you need. Like the Karate Kid's Mr. Miyagi, Jesus won't tell you everything he's doing to form you along the way. Don't complain about the car, just wax it; don't whine about the fence, just paint it. Keep sanding the floor, and before you know it, karate kid, you'll be on the mat, in the tournament, doing the crane technique and hoisting the trophy.

"Go...and make disciples" (Matthew 28:19). He's talking to you.

Shaken, Not Stirred

It struck me recently how many things require shaking in our world. Whether it's a bottle of juice, a canister of whipped cream or a can of paint, one of the most popular directions on household items is to "shake well before using." That got me thinking about a verse I read in Hebrews: "His voice then shook the earth; but now he has promised, 'Yet once more I will shake not only the earth but also the heaven.' This phrase, 'Yet once more,' indicates the removal of what is shaken, as of what has been made, in order that what cannot be shaken may remain" (Hebrews 12:26–27).

When bad things happen, and God knows they do, I often get nervous thinking that my faith will be shaken. That need not be the case. In reality, tough times can be God's way of shaking me free from the false gods and worldly ways that I'm hanging on to. He's rattling me for my own good, so that I'll be left with the unshakeable—God, the beginning and end of my life.

What things in your life, what "false gods," is our Lord trying to shake out of you ? What areas turn your attention from him? It's good when God points them out. It shows that he loves you enough to shake you out of the false loves and seductive lures of this world that lead to nothing but emptiness. The challenge is not to freak out when the shaking comes—easier said than done. God promises that we will never be tried beyond our abilities; God does not set us up to fail (see 1 Corinthians 10:13).

Practically Speaking

One of the hallmarks of disciples is that they are disciplined. Discipline provides the order necessary for a student—a disciple—to learn. If you're the type of person who's all over the place, there are dozens of small things that you can do on a regular basis that will help you become more disciplined so that you can be a better disciple. Many of these are small and practical but they contribute to an interior sense of peace. Here are a dozen ideas just to get you thinking:

1. Make your bed daily.
2. Clean your bathroom every week.
3. Exercise daily, even if it's just a walk.
4. Clean out your car once a week.
5. Fold your clothes the minute they come out of the dryer.
6. Learn how to cook a new meal twice a month.
7. Once a month, finish one of those books on your nightstand.
8. Pray for five people daily beyond your family and friends.
9. Read the book of Proverbs for five minutes before leaving the house.
10. Find out something new about a coworker or classmate each day; ask questions.

11. Lay out your outfit the night before so that you're free to pray in the morning.
12. Try the crossword every day, even if you don't come close to finishing it.

These twelve steps might not appear all that new or even that relevant in helping your faith to deepen, but if you're faithful in these little things it could impact your sense of discipline when it comes to your faith.

Make sure you pray daily. Read the Bible daily. In this prayer time try simple postures, gestures and actions that will help you enter more deeply into prayer. Lift and open your hands as a sign of your openness to God. Sing hymns. At Mass, spend time in sincere preparation before the liturgy starts. While you're at it, make every effort to sit closer to the front of the church—proximity often has a direct effect on attentiveness.

Finally, to help you develop the heart of a disciple, listen to uplifting or even educational CDs in your car. If you're a talk radio junkie, shut off the radio on your way to work or school. Start the day with morning silence rather than morning talk. On that note, remember that God gave you two ears and one mouth. Use them proportionately when you pray: Two-to-one is a good listen-to-talk ratio when it comes to the student and Master relationship with God.

CHAPTER NINE

Catholicism: The Never-Ending Crossword

URING MY JUNIOR YEAR IN COLLEGE I LOOKED FORWARD TO one class in particular. Not because the professor was brilliant or I liked the subject—in fact, I didn't even buy the textbook. The truth is that I found this right-after-lunch Tuesday and Thursday lecture so boring that I always did a crossword puzzle rather than pay attention. I was amazed at how much I learned, struggling through those obscure clues!

Some years later it occurred to me that the spiritual life is like those puzzles I used to do. There's the up-and-down relationship between God and us. There's the left-to-right relationship between the world and us. Some questions are easy to answer but some are difficult. Sometimes we ask for help but most of the time we don't. If we do well, we want praise; if we fail we hide the evidence. Often we try to fit things into our lives that are not meant for the space (our soul), and we end up with a problem. The result? The space remains empty for a while or the answer throws everything else off.

So how do we approach the "puzzle" of our lives? Many attempt their crossword halfheartedly, safely living "in pencil." Living "in pen," however, testifies to the boldness and confidence that the Gospel requires. Unfortunately, many never even attempt their spiritual crossword fearing their ignorance, weakness or sin will lead to failure. Others avoid it because it takes too much time away from self.

If we're going to live out our daily crossword, how do we start? Let me give you a clue. The puzzle hangs on one word: love. Shakespeare wrote about it. Prophets spoke about it. Rock bands sing about it. Therapists endlessly discuss it. The media harps on it. God calls you to it. Christ lived it. The saints modeled it. The masses want it but often fail to attain it.

It seems like a hit-or-miss kind of thing unless we realize that love is rooted in the surrender of every aspect of our being to God. Once we surrender and accept the love of God, we are empowered to really love others, to get on with our lives, to fill in the crossword.

This surrender, however, requires three things, all made possible through the power of the Holy Spirit: admission, attitude and abandonment.

Admission

I remember when my grandma came over for the holidays. I could smell her perfume from down the street. I had to speak slowly. She called me by my siblings' names or the name of my dog. I became expert at faking excitement over socks emblazoned with cartoon figures. I sat and listened as she rattled off a long list of people who had died, fallen down, or been diagnosed with diseases that I then prayed I would never contract.

And why was I forced to clean my room if Grandma never went in there? The holiday cleaning of the room eclipsed the normal, everyday pick up that was supposed to take place. It wasn't enough that the clothes were in the hamper; they had to be washed and in the drawers. It wasn't enough that you could see the carpeting; you had to see the lines left by the vacuum. I was a bulldozer of efficiency, pushing everything into the closet until I could just manage to close the door. My room wasn't clean. I knew it, my parents knew it and if Grandma could have climbed stairs, she would have known it too. (Kids don't have clean rooms; they just have rooms with plenty of hiding places.)

Our spiritual closets can be something like my childhood closet. The church understands this and gives us every opportunity throughout the year to clean out our closets in the sacrament of reconciliation, as we've already discussed. The church even gives us special seasons—Lent and Advent—to clean out our closets for the holidays. Of course, some of our messiness has nothing to do with sin, and so there are other ways to keep the clutter out of our lives such as trimming back on activities that interfere with family life or prayer time.

If you want to truly surrender to God, it helps to acknowledge your messiness. Admitting that you're far from perfect is key, because this admission leaves you standing consciously transparent before God. The time for hide-and-seek is over. The don't ask / don't tell approach to God doesn't work. The God-is-merciful-so-it-doesn't-matter-what-I-do philosophy will leave you twisted. God knows you through and through anyway, so you might as well invite him in so that he can help you straighten up the mess. And if anyone ever tells you that Holy Spirit couldn't possibly dwell within you because of your sin, tell him to hit the ATM, find the nearest mall and buy a clue.

Jesus left the glory and perfection of heaven to dwell in the sin, filth and imperfection of earth. He worked in the heat, walked in the dirt and slept on the ground. He reached out to lepers, healed paralytics and unleashed demons into swine. This is not someone afraid to get his hands dirty. He's ready to wade into your mess if you open the door to him.

Once you admit that your spiritual closet is cluttered, you're ready for the next question: Do you need an attitude adjustment?

Attitude

The circumstances of the day often dictate our attitude. Hunger, stress and fatigue are just a few that carry a punch. When circumstances rule, though, we set ourselves up for failure. One phone call, one jerk in traffic, one missed meal or one headache and we let the entire day unravel around us.

"Have no anxiety about anything...," Saint Paul tells us (Philippians 4:6). Don't let fear or anger or any of the other negative attitudes drive your day. It's OK to be concerned; it's OK to be appropriately angry so that you address a situation that needs correcting—a good attitude can work with that. It's when you're consumed by the worries and negative circumstances that you lose all logic, peace, perspective and common sense.

What should your attitude be? Move through daily life as if you are not going to screw up. Use the Holy Spirit as your guide and your strength, not your personal worry-stone. Live out what Scripture affirms: "I can do all things in him who strengthens me" (Philippians 4:13). Carry out your mission: "[B]e blameless and innocent, children of God without blemish in the midst of a crooked and perverse generation, among whom you shine as lights in the world..." (Philippians 2:15).

And when you feel that in the manger of life you're the hay covered with dung, remember how Jesus identified the truly blessed: those who are poor in spirit, who mourn, are meek, who hunger for righteousness, are merciful, pure in heart, peacemakers and persecuted (see Matthew 5:3–11).

Christ gives us these beatitudes because he wants these to be our attitudes. I read this passage often because I am often in need of an attitude adjustment. The blessed are not the impatient, the annoyed, the powerful, proud, snobby, cruel or self-centered but those who seek him in all things. You can do that. You'll fall short but you shouldn't set out to do so. Use the sacrament of reconciliation as a gift, not a pass. Pray a sincere prayer from your heart. Offer yourself to the Spirit, abandoning yourself to God.

Abandonment

The bags were loaded. The plane was oversold. My heart was beating out of my seventeen-year-old chest as I boarded the winged germ tube one hot August day and headed off to college alone. That's right, alone. No "Hey, we'll come and help you set up." No "You have eight hundred pounds of stuff to move in; we'll be there to lighten the load." Not for me. No, I received a tearful hug from Mom, a hearty handshake from Dad, a pocketful of cash, a ticket and warm wishes for a good semester.

I leaned back into my seat feeling uneasy and abandoned. Campus was over two thousand miles away from home. I didn't know a soul. I had never lived on my own. There was no one there to take care of me, to watch out for me, to ask me where I was going, to tell me what time to be home, to force me to go to class—wait, why was this a bad thing? Maybe abandonment had a bright side.

Seriously, though, there is another kind of abandonment that is at the heart of the spiritual life: when we forsake all else for that which is true. To abandon yourself to God means living for God when the feelings subside. It means putting Christ first in all things. It means trusting that he knows what he's doing, that he sees beyond your own limited horizons. It was overcast and raining when I left for college, a rare day in the usually sunny Phoenix. I remember feeling downcast, consumed by heaviness and anxiety. But once we took off and the plane broke through the clouds, there was brilliant sunlight above the blanket of gray. It was as though God was saying to me, "You exist only according to what you see, but this...this is how I see."

I needed far more than a change in altitude or attitude, though. I needed courage to abandon myself once and for all to God. I didn't do it then, unfortunately, and sin, mistakes and pain followed.

What more is it going to take? What does God have to do before you to take that final step and abandon your life to him? Ask yourself the question and then verbalize the answer to God in prayer. Don't just meditate on it; say it out loud. Not for his benefit, but for your own.

This last step in the quest for surrender can be the most difficult one. It was for me. I had reached the point where I could admit my sinfulness and knew that I had to change my attitude. But total abandonment to the Holy Spirit was the real leap. What are you prepared to do for God? Are you willing to be uncomfortable or lonely? Are you willing to forego financial security? Are you willing to move, to change or to start over at this stage in your life? If not, admit it. If so, you're ready to abandon yourself to God.

At this point, some run in the opposite direction, others stop and some courageously battle forward. I've seen the looks in the eyes and the resolve in the legs of those who do continue ahead. They walk through the mockery of classmates and coworkers. They dance while others sit. They drink from the cup of life that God reserves for those who trust him. They might not have the most money, but they do have the most power. They are the ones who decide to forge ahead with the crossword of life.

In the end, it's going to be between you and God. If you fear what he might say, change. If you don't, stay humble and faithful. If you're not sure, think harder. Come to terms with who you are, the good and the bad. Repent, reconcile and rejoice. When you do, you will have surrendered yourself. You will have admitted who you are and are not, changed your attitude and abandoned yourself to God.

The Truth About Love

Love is not a feeling; happiness is a feeling. Love is not an emotion; anger is an emotion. Love is not a state; confusion is a state. Love can include feeling and emotion and leave you in a state, but love is, at heart, a decision. Love sees the imperfections, sins and failings and says, "I still choose to love you."

The world says, "Love means never having to say you are sorry." Now that is a lie. As any married couple will attest, love means having to say you're sorry a lot.

The world says, "Love is give and take." That's half right. Love is give. We add "and take" out of fear. We fear that the other is not going to love us back or that they might take advantage of the love we offer. We fear we'll be left with nothing in return. There's nothing "and take" about the cross, however, and that's where we find our best example of love.

The world says, "Love is priceless." Not true. Love carries a heavy price, but Jesus picked up the tab for you and for me.

The world tells us, "Love doesn't come in a box." Yes it does. Love dwells in the tabernacle of every church, waiting for us to worship and adore, to find consolation and strength.

The world tells us, "Love doesn't grow on trees," but love grew out of a tree on Calvary that day when Jesus' blood watered the earth.

God doesn't love you because he is bored, nor does he just have loving feelings for his creation. God is love and when we love as he loves, we know him and live in him:

"God is love, and he who abides in love abides in God…" (1 John 4:16). Love frees you from being the center of the universe, and it means that the person you love is not the center of your world. Love means that God is your center, your air, and you cannot live without him nor would you want to. Love of God puts every other relationship into proper perspective.

Love is messy. It involves hardship, demands patience, requires forgiveness, tests maturity, strains friendship, challenges priorities, refines character, ignites the heart and unleashes the soul. True love has consequences and carries responsibility. It isn't the same as lust, looniness or severe "like." It means death to self, to selfishness and to the world.

The truth is that God doesn't just love you; he likes you. His greatest hope is that you will live for him and that he might live in you. There are people in this world whose only experience of Christ's mercy and love will be what they experience in you. Affirm their goodness. Serve them. Remind them of God's plan for their life. Never give up on yourself or on anyone else.

Even in passing and seemingly inconsequential ways, your life makes a difference every minute of every day. The Lord is asking you, directly, "Do you want to be part of the solution in this crossword or part of the problem, an empty space?" God sets before you the choice to follow him or to reject him, to make the choices that will build up or to make the choices that will tear down, to bring life or to destroy it. What mark will your life leave on the world today?

> I call heaven and earth to witness against you this day,
> that I have set before you life and death, blessing and
> curse; therefore choose life, that you and your descen-
> dants may live, loving the Lord your God, obeying his
> voice, and cleaving to him; for that means life to you and
> length of days.... (Deuteronomy 30:19–20)

Practically Speaking

Let's review what we've covered in this book. If we can
change our perspective of God, the way we approach our
God will change. This means that our encounter with Jesus
Christ will change, and this will be evident in how we
approach him at Mass, in the sacrament of reconciliation
and on a daily basis. Our perspective of suffering and our
understanding of the meaning of courage will also change,
rooted as they now are in an eternal perspective. Opening
ourselves to the Holy Spirit is essential if God is to form us
and use us as his disciples. And his mission for us means
that others encounter God's love in us and through us.

If you haven't had that transformation, you can.

If you don't live in awe, you will—*when* depends
on you.

If Mass is still just an obligation, it doesn't have to be.
Look again.

If your body is still "yours," think again.

If it's still confession, reconcile that idea and look
deeply into the mirror.

If sex is outside the parameters established by God,
make the changes you need to make.

If you're fearful or immersed in suffering, have courage;

don't lose your perspective.

If you're a disciple, be sure you keep learning.

If your life is one big puzzle, love. If it isn't a puzzle, love even more.

Take a step out in faith. When life doesn't make sense, rejoice in it anyway. It won't make sense entirely until we get home to heaven.

Take comfort in the fact that there are other believers who have experienced the same ups and downs, joys and fears in their faith as you, including plenty of saints. If the Lord pushed, pulled or provoked through these pages, thank him for that gift. But don't ignore it. Don't deny the stirrings of the Holy Spirit within you. Go to him in the fullness of your Catholic faith and reconnect with the Father, Son and Holy Spirit.

Choose life that you may live.

Be God's.

Chapter Two
Dumb as an Oxymoron: The Fear of the Lord
1. Mike Yaconelli, *Dangerous Wonder* (Colorado Springs: NavPress, 1998), p. 111.

Chapter Three
Mass Chaos: A Holy Day of Opportunity
1. Alan Schreck, *The Essential Catholic Catechism* (Cincinnati: Servant Books, 1999), p. 238.
2. Mary Healy, *Men and Women Are From Eden: A Study Guide to John Paul II's Theology of the Body* (Cincinnati: Servant Books, 2005), p. 68.

Chapter Five
Reconciling Your Issues: Thinking Inside the Box
1. Source: Crossroads Initiative library: http://www.crossroadsinitiative.com/library_article/212/Prayer_of_Abandonment__Charles_de_Foucauld.html

Chapter Six
Recreational Sex: Living in the Flesh
1. Healy, p. 3.
2. Fulton Sheen, *The Seven Words of Jesus and Mary* (Liguori, Missouri: Liguori, 2001), p. 89.
3. Pope John Paul II, Prayer Vigil, 15th World Youth Day, Tor Vergata, Italy, August 19, 2000, www.vatican.va.

Chapter Eight
Student Counsel: More Than a Popularity Contest
1. As adapted from *Hot Illustrations for Youth Talks on CD-Rom*, compiled by Wayne Rice (Grand Rapids, Mich.: Zondervan, 2001).